本書の構成と利用法

それぞれのパートは見開き 2 ページで構成されています。

見開きの左ページ

Ⓐ 新出単語を主な対象として，単語の意味もしくは英語を書かせる問題です。
A1〜B2は，CEFR-J でのレベルを表します。A1（易）〜B2（難）です。

Ⓑ 新出単語を主な対象とした発音問題もしくはアクセント問題です。

Ⓒ 重要な表現や文法に関する空所補充問題です。

Ⓓ 重要な表現や文法に関する語句整序問題です。

見開きの右ページ

Ⓔ 教科書本文の理解を確認する問題です。適語選択や語形変化，語句整序，英問英答など，多様な形式の問題を用意しました。

※本文中のグレーの網かけは，教科書では印字されておらず，音声としてのみ配信している部分であることを示します。

『CEFR-J Wordlist Version 1.6』東京外国語大学投野由紀夫研究室．（URL: http://cefr-j.org/download.html より2021年 2 月ダウンロード）

Japanese Athletes and English Part 1

/50

A Translate the English into Japanese and the Japanese into English. 【語彙の知識】(各1点)

1. proficient 形   [   ]   2. _____ 動 A2   …を続ける

3. furthermore 副 B1   [   ]   4. _____ 名 A2   ラップ(音楽)

5. _____ 動 A2   …を発音する   6. fluent 形 B1   [   ]

B Choose the word which has primary stress on a different syllable from the other three. 【アクセントの知識】   (各2点)

1. ア. ath-lete   イ. flu-ent   ウ. meth-od   エ. pro-nounce

2. ア. bas-ket-ball   イ. con-tin-ue   ウ. dis-cov-er   エ. per-form-ance

3. ア. ad-van-tage   イ. con-trib-ute   ウ. fur-ther-more   エ. pro-fi-cient

C Complete the following English sentences to match the Japanese. 【表現と文法の知識】

      (各3点)

1. 彼女は3か国語に堪能だ。

   She is (   ) (   ) three languages.

2. 私は床で眠ろうとしたがだめだった。

   I (   ) (   ) (   ) on the floor, but I couldn't.

3. 彼はその単語の発音を何度も練習した。

   He practiced pronouncing the word (   ) (   )
   (   ).

D Arrange the words in the proper order to match the Japanese. 【表現と文法の知識・技能】

      (各3点)

1. 自転車に乗っているときにスマートフォンを使ってはいけない。

   You must not use your smartphone (are / riding / while / you) a bike.

_____

2. 先生は授業中私たちによく冗談を言った。

   The teacher (jokes / often / told / us) in class.

_____

3. お兄さんはその仕事を引き受けることに決めたのですか。

   (decide / did / to / your brother) take the job?

_____

E Read the following passage and answer the questions below.

Today, many Japanese athletes are playing sports in various countries around the world. They show us great performances, and some of (1) are also proficient in English. One of those athletes is Rui Hachimura, an NBA player.

In high school, Rui was not good (2) English. In his third year, he decided to play basketball at an American university. From that time, he continued to study English very hard.

At university, Rui (3)(take) an ESL course. Furthermore, he discovered his own English-learning method. One day, while he was listening to English rap songs, he started trying to pronounce the words as they sounded. Then, he repeated (4)this again and again. Rui (5)(speak) fluent English now.

1. 空所(1), (2)に入る最も適当な語を選びなさい。【語彙と表現の知識】　　　　　　(各2点)

(1) ア. their　　　　イ. theirs　　　　ウ. them　　　　エ. they

(2) ア. at　　　　イ. in　　　　ウ. on　　　　エ. to

2. 下線部(3), (5)の語を適切な形に変えなさい。【文法の知識】　　　　　　　　　(各2点)

(3) ....

(5) ....

3. 下線部(4)は何を指していますか。日本語で答えなさい。【内容についての思考力・判断力・表現力】

(4点)

....

4. 次の問いに英語で答えなさい。【内容についての思考力・判断力・表現力】　　　(各4点)

(1) What did Rui decide when he was in his third year in high school?

....

(2) When did Rui discover his own English-learning method?

....

A Translate the English into Japanese and the Japanese into English.【語彙の知識】(各1点)

1. _____ 名　新人選手
2. entire 形 B1　[　　　　　　　　]
3. _____ 形　無条件の
4. _____ 名 B1　未来像，展望
5. encouragement 名 B1　[　　　　　　　]
6. hopefully 副 B1　[　　　　　　　]

B Choose the word whose underlined part is pronounced differently from the other three.【発音の知識】(各2点)

1. ア. b<u>a</u>tter　　イ. f<u>a</u>mous　　ウ. m<u>a</u>jor　　エ. st<u>a</u>ge
2. ア. c<u>o</u>ming　　イ. disc<u>o</u>ver　　ウ. h<u>o</u>pefully　　エ. <u>o</u>ther
3. ア. ch<u>ea</u>t　　イ. gr<u>ea</u>t　　ウ. n<u>ee</u>d　　エ. sh<u>ee</u>t

C Complete the following English sentences to match the Japanese.【表現と文法の知識】

(各3点)

1. 彼らは彼の成功を信頼し続け，彼を支援し続けた。

They kept (　　　　　) (　　　　　　) his success and continued supporting him.

2. 私はこの記憶に残る賞を受賞して光栄に思います。

I am (　　　　　) (　　　　　　) receive this memorable prize.

3. その情報を私たちと共有してくれますか。

Can you (　　　　　　) the information (　　　　　　) us?

D Arrange the words in the proper order to match the Japanese.【表現と文法の知識・技能】

(各3点)

1. 今日映画を見に行くのはどう？

(about / going / to / what) the movies today?

_____

2. 昨年，彼女はスピーチコンテストで1位を受賞した。

Last year, (awarded / first prize / she / was) in the speech contest.

_____

3. 次に会うときに返事をちょうだい。

Give me your answer the (I / next / see / time) you.

_____

E Read the following passage and answer the questions below.

(1) *2018, Shohei was awarded the Rookie of the Year Award. He attended a party with other prize winners, and he* (2)(*say*) *the following words in his speech.*

I am honored to share this stage with so many great players. Congratulations to you all. I would like to say some special thank-yous.

To the entire Angels organization for their unconditional support and believing in me and my vision. To my teammates for their support and encouragement. To my parents for (3)(come) from Japan to be here tonight. (4), to all the Angels fans, thank you.

Hopefully, I (5)(cheat sheet / need / not / this / will) the next time I'm up here. Thank you.

1. 空所(1)に入る最も適当な語を選びなさい。【語彙の知識】 （2点）

　　ア. At　　　　　イ. For　　　　　ウ. In　　　　　エ. On

2. 下線部(2), (3)の語を適切な形に変えなさい。【文法の知識】 （各2点）

　　(2) ⋯⋯⋯⋯⋯⋯⋯⋯⋯⋯⋯⋯⋯⋯⋯⋯⋯

　　(3) ⋯⋯⋯⋯⋯⋯⋯⋯⋯⋯⋯⋯⋯⋯⋯⋯⋯

3. 空所(4)に入る最も適当な語(句)を選びなさい。【語彙と表現の知識】 （3点）

　　ア. Firstly　　　　イ. For example　　ウ. However　　　エ. Lastly

4. 下線部(5)の(　　)内の語句を適切に並べかえなさい。【表現と文法の知識】 （3点）

5. 次の問いに英語で答えなさい。【内容についての思考力・判断力・表現力】 （各4点）

　　(1) What was Shohei awarded at this party?

　　(2) Who gave Shohei support and encouragement?

A Translate the English into Japanese and the Japanese into English.【語彙の知識】(各1点)

1. _____ 名 A2　発音　　2. attractive 形 A2　[　　　　　]

3. _____ 名 B1　感謝の気持ち　4. probably 副 A2　[　　　　　]

5. ability 名 A2　[　　　　　]　6. _____ 動　(言葉)を自由に操る

B Choose the word which has primary stress on a different syllable from the other three.【アクセントの知識】(各2点)

1. ア. com-mand　イ. con-cern　ウ. im-prove　エ. mes-sage

2. ア. at-trac-tive　イ. grat-i-tude　ウ. prob-a-bly　エ. rec-og-nize

3. ア. con-grat-u-la-tion　イ. or-gan-i-za-tion　ウ. pro-nun-ci-a-tion　エ. un-con-di-tion-al

C Complete the following English sentences to match the Japanese.【表現の知識】(各3点)

1. お年寄りを敬うべきだ。

You should (　　　　) your (　　　　) to elderly people.

2. 彼の息子は父親にそっくりだ。

His son looks (　　　　) (　　　　) his father.

3. 母は今そのプロジェクトに一生懸命取り組んでいる。

My mother is (　　　　) (　　　　) (　　　　) the project now.

D Arrange the words in the proper order to match the Japanese.【表現と文法の知識・技能】(各3点)

1. 私は母の健康を心配しています。

I (about / am / concerned / my mother's health).

2. 彼女はその絵がいかに素晴らしかったかについて何度も話をした。

She talked again and again about (how / that painting / was / wonderful).

3. 彼女は子供たちに囲まれて座っているときに幸せを感じた。

She felt happy when (by / sat / she / surrounded) her children.

E Read the following passage and answer the questions below.

When you hear Japanese athletes' English, you may be concerned about their pronunciation. However, (1)(else / even / is / more important / something): how attractive their messages are.

Take Shohei's speech, for example. He did not talk only about himself. At the beginning, he congratulated the other award winners. They were also (2)(recognize) for their great performances, so he showed his respect to (3)those players. Then, Shohei expressed his gratitude to the team, fans and his parents. At the end, he even (4)(make) a joke!

Probably, most of you work hard on your club activities and English learning, just like many Japanese athletes. Keep (5)(try) to improve your skills in your clubs and your ability to command English.

1. 下線部(1)の(　　)内の語句を適切に並べかえなさい。【表現の知識】　　　　　（3点）

　　　

2. 下線部(2), (4), (5)の語を適切な形に変えなさい。【文法の知識】　　　　　　（各2点）

　　(2)

　　(4)

　　(5)

3. 下線部(3)は何を指していますか。英語で答えなさい。【内容についての思考力・判断力・表現力】

　　（3点）

　　　

4. 次の問いに英語で答えなさい。【内容についての思考力・判断力・表現力】　　　（各4点）

　　(1) Did Shohei only talk about himself?

　　　

　　(2) Who did Shohei express his gratitude to?

A Translate the English into Japanese and the Japanese into English.【語彙の知識】(各1点)

1. _____ 名　調味料　　2. _____ 名 A2　コショウ

3. contain 動 B1　[　　　　　]　4. _____ 名　カリウム

5. blood 名 A2　[　　　　　]　6. _____ 名 B1　絶滅

B Choose the word which has primary stress on a different syllable from the other three.【アクセントの知識】(各2点)

1. ア. ba-nan-a　　イ. dif-fer-ent　　ウ. fa-mil-iar　　エ. gym-nas-tics

2. ア. Can-a-da　　イ. con-ven-ience　　ウ. min-er-al　　エ. vi-ta-min

3. ア. com-mon　　イ. com-pete　　ウ. con-tain　　エ. cre-ate

C Complete the following English sentences to match the Japanese.【表現と文法の知識】

(各3点)

1. トミーの話は筋が通っている。彼は真実を話しているようだ。

Tommy's stories make sense.　He (　　　　　) (　　　　　)
(　　　　　) (　　　　　) the truth.

2. 望美は英語だけでなく中国語も話せる。

Nozomi can speak Chinese (　　　　　) (　　　　　) (　　　　　)
English.

3. 台風のせいで修学旅行が中止になった。

Our school trip was called off (　　　　　) (　　　　　) the typhoon.

D Arrange the words in the proper order to match the Japanese.【表現の知識・技能】(各3点)

1. パンケーキは小麦粉，砂糖，卵を使って作られる。

Pancakes (are / flour / made / with), sugar, and eggs.

_____

2. ラッコは絶滅の危機にさらされている。

Sea otters (are / danger / extinction / in / of).

_____

3. 納豆が健康によいということは多くの日本人が知っていることだ。

Many Japanese know that (for / good / health / is / natto / our).

_____

E Read the following passage and answer the questions below.

People around the world seem to love bananas. In the Philippines, sweet fried bananas are a common street food. Puerto Ricans make a hot banana soup. (1)It is made with some seasonings, such as salt and black pepper. Different (2)(cultures / different / have / own / their / ways) of eating this delicious fruit.

Bananas are good for our health as well as delicious. They contain a good amount of vitamins and minerals. One of the minerals is potassium. This mineral is useful in (3)(lower) blood pressure.

Bananas are very familiar to people all over the world. (4), this fruit is in danger of extinction due to a disease.

1. 下線部(1)は何を指していますか。英語で答えなさい。【内容についての思考力・判断力・表現力】（3点）

2. 下線部(2)の(   )内の語を適切に並べかえなさい。【表現の知識】　　　　　　　（3点）

3. 下線部(3)の語を適切な形に変えなさい。【文法の知識】　　　　　　　　　　　　（3点）

4. 空所(4)に入る最も適当な語を選びなさい。【語彙と表現の知識】　　　　　　　　（3点）
    ア. Besides　　　　　イ. However　　　　ウ. Moreover　　　　エ. Therefore

5. 次の問いに英語で答えなさい。【内容についての思考力・判断力・表現力】　　　（各4点）
    (1) What do people around the world seem to love?

    (2) What contains a good amount of vitamins and minerals?

Our Beloved Yellow Fruit

Part 2

/50

A Translate the English into Japanese and the Japanese into English.【語彙の知識】(各1点)

1. risk 名 B1　　　　　[　　　　　　]　2. ＿＿＿＿＿＿ 動 B2　…に伝染する

3. ＿＿＿＿＿＿ 名 B2　細菌, ばい菌　4. plantation 名　　[　　　　　　]

5. resistant 形　　　[　　　　　　]　6. ＿＿＿＿＿＿ 動 B2　…をおびやかす

B Choose the word which has primary stress on a different syllable from the other three.【アクセントの知識】(各2点)

1. ア. a-muse-ment　　イ. at-ten-tion　　ウ. Jap-a-nese　　エ. spe-cif-ic

2. ア. Gha-nai-an　　イ. Ha-wai-ian　　ウ. Pan-a-ma　　エ. I-tal-ian

3. ア. girl-friend　　イ. he-ro　　ウ. per-cent　　エ. threat-en

C Complete the following English sentences to match the Japanese.【表現と文法の知識】(各3点)

1. 風邪を引いてしまった。エアコンのせいだ。

I've got a cold. It (　　　　　) (　　　　　) by air conditioner.

2. コウノトリの将来は危険にさらされている。

The future of storks is (　　　　　) (　　　　　).

3. この建物は地震に耐性がある。

This building (　　　　　) (　　　　　) (　　　　　) earthquakes.

D Arrange the words in the proper order to match the Japanese.【表現と文法の知識・技能】(各3点)

1. 政府は核兵器の開発をしないようにしている。

The government (avoids / nuclear weapons / of / production / the).

2. 鬼塚先生はナンシーという名前の新しい ALT を紹介した。

Mr. Onitsuka (a / ALT / introduced / Nancy / named / new).

3. 早寝早起きは健康によい。

(for / good / health / is / it / keep / to / your) early hours.

E Read the following passage and answer the questions below.

The future of bananas is now at risk due to Panama disease. This disease infects banana plants from their roots and finally kills them. It is caused by a specific kind of germ.

People once enjoyed a delicious kind of banana (1)(name) Gros Michel. This kind was produced mainly in Central and South America. In the 1950s, however, Panama disease attacked almost all the banana plantations there, and Gros Michel nearly became extinct. (2), people began to produce another type of banana called Cavendish. It was resistant (3) Panama disease.

Again, however, a new type of Panama disease began to infect bananas. This disease is now threatening the production of even Cavendish. (4)It is difficult for modern technologies to stop the disease.

1. 下線部(1)の語を適切な形に変えなさい。【文法の知識】　　　　　　　　　　（4点）

2. 空所(2), (3)に入る最も適当な語を選びなさい。【語彙と表現の知識】　　　　（各2点）
   (2) ア. Besides　　イ. However　　ウ. Instead　　エ. Thus
   (3) ア. at　　　　イ. for　　　　ウ. on　　　　エ. to

3. 下線部(4)の文の意味上の主語を英語で答えなさい。【表現と文法の知識】　　　（4点）

4. 次の問いに英語で答えなさい。【内容についての思考力・判断力・表現力】　　（各4点）
   (1) Where was Gros Michel produced mainly?

   (2) Why did Gros Michel nearly become extinct?

Our Beloved Yellow Fruit

Part 3

/50

A Translate the English into Japanese and the Japanese into English.【語彙の知識】(各1点)

1. _____ 形 B2　同源の，同根の　　2. gene 名 B1　　[　　　　　　　]

3. _____ 名 B1　伝染病，伝染症　　4. exist 動 A2　　[　　　　　　　]

5. effective 形 B1　[　　　　　　]　　6. _____ 動 B2　…を操作する

B Choose the word which has primary stress on a different syllable from the other three.【アクセントの知識】

(各2点)

1. ア. hap-pen　　　イ. lis-ten　　　　ウ. pre-vent　　　エ. shak-en

2. ア. di-am-e-ter　　イ. i-den-ti-cal　　ウ. in-ac-cu-rate　　エ. math-e-mat-ics

3. ア. in-fec-tion　　イ. li-brar-y　　　ウ. mu-si-cian　　　エ. per-form-ance

C Complete the following English sentences to match the Japanese.【表現と文法の知識】

(各3点)

1. 新しい言語を学ぶのは大変です。

(　　　　　　) (　　　　　　　) hard (　　　　　　) learn a new language.

2.「なんで英語を勉強するの？」「理由の一つは海外に留学したいからだよ。」

"Why do you study English?"　"(　　　　　　) (　　　　　　) is

(　　　　　　) I want to study abroad."

3. よりよい未来のために何か私たちにできることはありますか。

Is there (　　　　　　) we can do for a better future?

D Arrange the words in the proper order to match the Japanese.【表現と文法の知識・技能】

(各3点)

1. 私に嘘をつこうとしているの？

(a lie / are / tell / to / trying / you) to me?

2. 下村先生は私たちに数学の効果的な勉強法を教えてくれた。

Ms. Shimomura (effective / math / study / taught / to / us / ways).

3. 私はサンタクロースがいると本当に信じています。

(believe / do / I / in / Santa Claus).

E Read the following passage and answer the questions below.

Vivian: (1)(hard / is / it / Panama disease / prevent / to / why)?

Mr. Tanaka: Well, one reason is that most bananas on the earth have identical genes. If one banana plant is infected by a germ, the infection can easily spread to the rest in the area.

Vivian: (2)

Mr. Tanaka: Besides this, the germs exist in the ground. (3)They can move quickly from one area to another through the soil.

Vivian: Is there (4) we can do?

Mr. Tanaka: Scientists are now trying to find effective ways to save bananas. One of the ways is to manipulate the genes of bananas.

Vivian: I do hope our beloved fruit will stay with us forever!

1. 下線部(1)の(　　)内の語を適切に並べかえなさい。【文法の知識】　　　　　（3点）

2. 空所(2)に入る最も適当な表現を選びなさい。【表現の知識】　　　　　　　　　（3点）
　　ア. I don't agree with you.　　　　イ. Oh, dear.
　　ウ. Sounds good.　　　　　　　　エ. Wonderful!

3. 下線部(3)は何を指していますか。英語で答えなさい。【内容についての思考力・判断力・表現力】（3点）

4. 空所(4)に入る最も適当な語を選びなさい。【語彙の知識】　　　　　　　　　　（3点）
　　ア. anything　　　　イ. everything　　　ウ. thing　　　　　エ. ways

5. 次の問いに英語で答えなさい。【内容についての思考力・判断力・表現力】　　　　（各4点）
　　(1) What can happen if one banana plant is infected by a germ in some area?

　　(2) What is one of the ways to save bananas?

Preparing for Potential Risks

Part 1

/50

A Translate the English into Japanese and the Japanese into English.【語彙の知識】(各1点)

1. _____ 名 B1　損害，被害
2. average 形 A2　[　　　　　]
3. _____ 名 B1　犠牲者，被災者
4. sharply 副 B2　[　　　　　]
5. flood 名 A2　[　　　　　]
6. _____ 動 A2　…を予想する

B Choose the word whose underlined part is pronounced differently from the other three.【発音の知識】(各2点)

1. ア. fl<u>oo</u>d　　イ. t<u>oo</u>　　ウ. typh<u>oo</u>n　　エ. z<u>oo</u>

2. ア. <u>a</u>verage　　イ. d<u>a</u>mage　　ウ. dis<u>a</u>ster　　エ. sc<u>a</u>le

3. ア. c<u>o</u>st　　イ. <u>o</u>ver　　ウ. p<u>o</u>st　　エ. r<u>o</u>se

C Complete the following English sentences to match the Japanese.【表現と文法の知識】(各3点)

1. 天気予報によると，明日は雨のようだ。

(　　　　　) (　　　　　　　　) the weather forecast, it will rain tomorrow.

2. この建物は何年もの間変わっていない。

This building (　　　　　) (　　　　　　　) the same for many years.

3. 自転車事故の数は年々増加している。

The number of bicycle accidents has increased (　　　　　) (　　　　　)
(　　　　　).

D Arrange the words in the proper order to match the Japanese.【表現と文法の知識・技能】(各3点)

1. スピーチをするときに緊張するのは当然だ。

It is (are / natural / that / you) nervous when you make a speech.

2. 火事の場合はそのドアから出てください。

Go out the door (a / case / fire / in / of).

3. 具合が悪いのは当たり前だよ。食べ過ぎだよ。

It's (not / surprising / that / you) are sick. You ate too much.

E Read the following passage and answer the questions below.

The graph shows that the amount of damage (1)(cause) by natural disasters increased year by year. The average number of disasters rose more than eight times during a 30-year period. According to the graph, the number of victims (2)(rise) sharply in the period of 1987–1991 and remained around 200 million. The cost of damage also increased. (3)It reached well over 100 billion dollars in the period of 2007–2011.

Earthquakes, typhoons and floods are becoming larger and larger in scale. Such natural disasters may hit us anytime. The damage can be (4) than you expect. It is important that you (5)(know / need / what / will / you) in case of a disaster.

Thank you.

1. 下線部(1), (2)の語を適切な形に変えなさい。【文法の知識】　　　　　　　　（各2点）

　　(1) ....

　　(2) ....

2. 下線部(3)は何を指していますか。英語で答えなさい。【内容についての思考力・判断力・表現力】（3点）

　　..

3. 空所(4)に入る最も適当な語(句)を選びなさい。【語彙と表現の知識】　　　　　　（2点）

　　ア. more much severe　　イ. much more severe　　ウ. much severe　　エ. severe

4. 下線部(5)の(　　)内の語を適切に並べかえなさい。【表現と文法の知識】　　　（3点）

　　..

5. 次の問いに英語で答えなさい。【内容についての思考力・判断力・表現力】　　　（各4点）

　　(1) What is becoming larger and larger in scale?

　　..

　　(2) What is important in case of a disaster?

　　..

Preparing for Potential Risks

Part 2

/50

A Translate the English into Japanese and the Japanese into English. 【語彙の知識】（各 1 点）

1. .... 形 B1　特有の，典型的な
2. region 名 B1　[　　　　　　　]
3. occur 動 B1　[　　　　　　　]
4. measure 名 B1　[　　　　　　　]
5. .... 名 B2　避難
6. .... 名 B1　意識

B Choose the word which has primary stress on a different syllable from the other three. 【アクセントの知識】　(各 2 点)

1. ア. earth-quake　　イ. haz-ard　　　ウ. oc-cur　　　エ. suf-fer
2. ア. lo-ca-tion　　　イ. po-ten-tial　　ウ. pre-ven-tive　エ. typ-i-cal
3. ア. a-ware-ness　　イ. gov-ern-ment　ウ. nat-u-ral　　エ. ter-ri-ble

C Complete the following English sentences to match the Japanese. 【表現と文法の知識】

(各 3 点)

1. 母はあまりにおしゃべりの傾向があり，私はそれが好きではない。

   My mother (　　　　　　) (　　　　　　　　) talk too much and I don't like it.
2. 薬物に関連した犯罪の数が増えている。

   The number of crimes (　　　　　　) (　　　　　　　) drugs has been increasing.
3. 私は何年もの間頭痛を患っている。

   I have (　　　　　　) (　　　　　　　) headaches for many years.

D Arrange the words in the proper order to match the Japanese. 【表現と文法の知識・技能】

(各 3 点)

1. 今晩雨が降りそうだ。

   It (is / likely / rain / to) this evening.

2. そのシャツをもう一度着たかったが，母がもう洗濯機に入れてしまっていた。

   I wanted to wear the shirt again, but (already / had / my mother / put) it in the washing machine.

3. ここに引っ越してくるまでは，こんなことは一度も起こったことはなかった。

   This (had / happened / never / to) me before I moved here.

E Read the following passage and answer the questions below.

Typical natural disasters are different from region to region. Severe storms and floods often happen in Asia. In Central and South America, huge earthquakes (1) to occur. In Africa, people tend to suffer from terrible droughts.

Japan (2) from earthquakes and typhoons many times. The Japanese government has collected data about damage caused by these disasters. By (3)(use) the data, it has introduced various measures to avoid potential risks related to disasters and has saved people's lives.

One effective measure is the use of hazard maps. These maps (4)(areas / be / can / show / that) affected by floods and earthquakes. (5)They also tell people the location of the nearest evacuation site in each area. The maps raise people's awareness of preventive measures against disasters.

1. 空所(1), (2)に入る最も適当な語句を選びなさい。【語彙と表現の知識】　　　　　　(各2点)

   (1) ア. are like　　イ. are likely　　ウ. like　　　　エ. likely

   (2) ア. has been suffered　　　　　イ. has suffered

     ウ. has suffering　　　　　　　エ. suffering

2. 下線部(3)の語を適切な形に変えなさい。【文法の知識】　　　　　　　　　　　(2点)

3. 下線部(4)の(　　)内の語を適切に並べかえなさい。【文法の知識】　　　　　(3点)

4. 下線部(5)は何を指していますか。日本語で答えなさい。【内容についての思考力・判断力・表現力】

 (3点)

5. 次の問いに英語で答えなさい。【内容についての思考力・判断力・表現力】　　　(各4点)

   (1) What are the typical natural disasters in Africa?

   (2) What has the Japanese government introduced?

Preparing for Potential Risks

Part 3

/50

A Translate the English into Japanese and the Japanese into English.【語彙の知識】(各1点)

1. ＿＿＿＿＿ 名 体育館
2. arise 動 B1 [   ]
3. loss 名 B1 [   ]
4. ＿＿＿＿＿ 名 B1 不快感
5. ＿＿＿＿＿ 副 B2 劇的に
6. survive 動 A2 [   ]

B Choose the word whose underlined part is pronounced differently from the other three.【発音の知識】(各2点)

1. ア. am<u>ou</u>nt   イ. dr<u>ou</u>ght   ウ. h<u>o</u>wever   エ. <u>ow</u>n
2. ア. d<u>e</u>pend   イ. m<u>ea</u>sure   ウ. r<u>e</u>gion   エ. t<u>e</u>nd
3. ア. dis<u>c</u>omfort   イ. eruption   ウ. <u>g</u>overnment   エ. lo<u>ss</u>

C Complete the following English sentences to match the Japanese.【表現と文法の知識】

(各3点)

1. 彼はあらゆることを母親に頼っている。

   He (   ) (   ) his mother for everything.

2. その問題はコミュニケーション不足から生じた。

   The problem (   ) (   ) a lack of communication.

3. 彼をスマートフォンから引き離すのは容易ではない。

   It is not easy to (   ) (   ) (   ) his smartphone.

D Arrange the words in the proper order to match the Japanese.【表現と文法の知識・技能】

(各3点)

1. 長時間歩くのには慣れています。

   I (am / to / used / walking) for long hours.

2. 私が現場に着いたとき，窃盗犯はすでに警察によって逮捕されていた。

   The robbers (already / arrested / been / had) by the police when I arrived at the scene.

3. これは今までにない発見だと思います。

   I think that this is a discovery that (been / has / not / made) yet.

E Read the following passage and answer the questions below.

Once a natural disaster happens, people rush to an evacuation site like a school gymnasium. Most people are not used to (1)(be) with strangers for a long time. They experience stress (2)(arise) from the loss of privacy.

Cardboard boxes (3)(been / have / relieve / to / used) such discomfort. By using (4)them, people are able to separate themselves from others. Also, cardboard box beds are helpful for keeping away the bitter cold in gyms.

Preventive measures against disasters have dramatically improved our chances of surviving (5)them. However, it depends on each of us to reduce our own risk in future disasters. It is never too early to get prepared for them.

1. 下線部(1)，(2)の語を適切な形に変えなさい。【文法の知識】　　　　　　　　　　　(各2点)

   (1) _____

   (2) _____

2. 下線部(3)の(　　)内の語を適切に並べかえなさい。【文法の知識】　　　　　　　(4 点)

_____

3. 下線部(4)，(5)は何を指していますか。英語で答えなさい。【内容についての思考力・判断力・表現力】

(各 2 点)

   (4) _____

   (5) _____

4. 次の問いに英語で答えなさい。【内容についての思考力・判断力・表現力】　　　(各4点)

  (1) What is helpful when we keep away the bitter cold in evacuation sites?

_____

  (2) For what should we get prepared early?

_____

To Make a More Open Society

Part 1

/50

A Translate the English into Japanese and the Japanese into English.【語彙の知識】(各1点)

1. schedule 名 A2   [   ]   2. demonstration 名 B1   [   ]

3. workshop 名 B1   [   ]   4. _____ 名 B1   入場料

5. _____ 名 B2   移民, 移住者   6. _____ 名 B2   居住者

B Choose the word which has primary stress on a different syllable from the other three.【アクセントの知識】

(各2点)

1. ア. cloth-ing   イ. sched-ule   ウ. up-set   エ. work-shop

2. ア. ad-mis-sion   イ. cul-tur-al   ウ. har-mo-ny   エ. im-mi-grant

3. ア. com-pe-ti-tion   イ. dem-on-stra-tion ウ. in-for-ma-tion   エ. tel-e-vi-sion

C Complete the following English sentences to match the Japanese.【表現と文法の知識】

(各3点)

1. 浴衣の着方を教えてもらえませんか。

   Could you teach us (   ) to (   ) *yukata*?

2. 大学生になったら留学するつもりです。

   I'm going to (   ) (   ) when I become a college student.

3. このお祭りはいつ開催されるか知っていますか。

   Do you know (   ) this festival will (   )
   (   )?

D Arrange the words in the proper order to match the Japanese.【表現の知識・技能】 (各3点)

1. 私はこの夏, 北海道を訪れる計画です。

   (Hokkaido / I'm / on / planning / visiting) this summer.

   _____

2. 試験に合格するために一生懸命勉強しなさい。

   (hard / in / must / order / pass / study / to / you) the exam.

   _____

3. 私は自然と調和した暮らしをしようと思う。

   I will try to (harmony / in / live / nature / with).

   _____

E Read the following passage and answer the questions below.

International Festival and Cultural Exchange
August 1 @Room 101, Daiichi Bldg.

Come to Learn about Your Neighbors!

Schedule
10:00-10:10 Opening
10:10-11:00 Japanese Cultural Demonstrations
11:00-12:00 International Fashion Show of Traditional Clothing
12:00-14:00 Lunch Buffet and Games
14:00-15:00 Workshop on How to Wear *Yukatas*
15:00-15:10 Closing

Come and join us. Everyone is welcome!

For more information, visit our website:

www.daiichi-ifce.org

Admission is free

Kumi: Hey, there's going to be an international festival (1) August 1. I'm planning on going.

David: Sounds good! In England (2)there are (   ) immigrants now. In order to live in harmony with each other, I often went to international exchange events there.

Kumi: Oh, I'm also interested in these kinds of events. (3)I'd (   ) to study abroad next year.

David: That's great!

Kumi: Perhaps foreign residents can tell me what I need to do before I go abroad.

David: Good luck, Kumi!

1. 空所(1)に入る最も適当な語を選びなさい。【語彙の知識】　　　　　　　　　　　　　　　（4点）

　　ア. at　　　　　　イ. in　　　　　　ウ. on　　　　　　エ. to

2. 下線部(2)が「今ではたくさんの移民がいる」という意味になるように，空所に入る表現をすべて選びなさい。【表現と語彙の知識】　　　　　　　　　　　　　　　（4点）

　　ア. a lot of　　　　イ. less　　　　　ウ. many　　　　　エ. much

3. 下線部(3)が「来年留学したい」という意味になるように，空所に適語を補いなさい。

　　　　　　　　　　　　　　　　　　　　　　　　　　　　　　　【表現の知識】（4点）

　　I'd (　　　　　　　　) to study abroad next year.

4. 次の問いに英語で答えなさい。【内容についての思考力・判断力・表現力】　　　　　　（各4点）

　　(1) To which room should you go to join the festival?

　　　　...

　　(2) Why did David go to international exchange events?

　　　　...

To Make a More Open Society   Part 2

/50

A Translate the English into Japanese and the Japanese into English.【語彙の知識】(各1点)

1. _____ 動   …を国際化する
2. _____ 名 B2   福祉
3. facility 名 B1   [   ]
4. devote 動 B2   [   ]
5. _____ 名 B2   同僚, 仲間
6. co-worker 名   [   ]

B Choose the word which has primary stress on a different syllable from the other three.【アクセントの知識】(各2点)

1. ア. a-broad   イ. en-joy   ウ. peo-ple   エ. to-day
2. ア. con-fer-ence   イ. con-ven-ience   ウ. fa-vor-ite   エ. in-dus-try
3. ア. de-vote   イ. mon-ey   ウ. nev-er   エ. wel-fare

C Complete the following English sentences to match the Japanese.【表現と文法の知識】(各3点)

1. きれいな花をあちこちで見ることができます。

   We can see beautiful flowers (   ) and (   ).

2. 美紀は両親の手伝いに献身的に尽くす。

   Miki (   ) herself to (   ) her parents.

3. 英語を勉強する人が増えています。

   The (   ) of people who study English is (   ).

D Arrange the words in the proper order to match the Japanese.【表現と文法の知識・技能】(各3点)

1. そのコンサートに参加した人はコンサートが始まるまで長時間待たないといけなかった。

   (attended / had / people / the concert / to / wait / who) for a long time before the concert began.

   _____

2. 健司は市の職員として働いている。

   Kenji (a / as / city / officer / serves).

   _____

3. 君が薦めてくれた本を読んだよ。

   I (read / recommended / that / the book / you).

   _____

E Read the following passage and answer the questions below.

Japan has become (1). People from abroad enjoy sightseeing all over the country. We also see foreign people (2)(and / and working / are studying / here / there / who).

At convenience stores in Japan, people from other countries serve as cashiers politely and with smiles. In welfare facilities, care workers from abroad devote themselves to helping elderly people. They are welcomed by the elderly because (3)they are kind and friendly toward them.

Another example is seen in IT industries. The number of people from abroad who work as advanced engineers and skilled programmers is increasing. They communicate well with their Japanese colleagues and do good work in their companies. Some of them instruct their co-workers (4) managers.

1. 空所(1)に入る最も適当な語を選びなさい。【語彙の知識】 （3点）

　　ア. independence 　　　　イ. internationalized 　　　ウ. internationalizing

2. 下線部(2)の( )内の語句を適切に並べかえなさい。【表現と文法の知識】 （3点）

　　..

3. 下線部(3)を they と them の指すものを明らかにして，日本語にしなさい。

　　【内容についての思考力・判断力・表現力】（3点）

　　..

4. 空所(4)を含む文が「中には管理者として同僚に指導をする人もいる」という意味になるように，適当な語を選びなさい。【表現の知識】 （3点）

　　ア. as 　　　　　イ. at 　　　　　ウ. in 　　　　　エ. with

5. 次の問いに英語で答えなさい。【内容についての思考力・判断力・表現力】 （各4点）

　　(1) How do people from other countries serve as cashiers at convenience stores in Japan?

　　..

　　(2) Can advanced engineers and skilled programmers from abroad communicate well with their Japanese colleagues?

　　..

To Make a More Open Society   Part 3

/50

A Translate the English into Japanese and the Japanese into English.【語彙の知識】(各1点)

1. benefit 名 B1　　　[　　　　　　]　　2. nowadays 副 A2　　[　　　　　　　]

3. workforce 名　　　[　　　　　　]　　4. _____ 名 B1　雰囲気, 空気

5. _____ 名 B1　多様性　　　　6. _____ 動 A2　成功する

B Choose the word which has primary stress on a different syllable from the other three.【アクセントの知識】(各2点)

1. ア. ben-e-fit　　イ. o-pen-ing　　ウ. o-pin-ion　　エ. pas-sen-ger

2. ア. con-fuse　　イ. sto-ry　　　ウ. walk-ing　　エ. work-force

3. ア. bet-ter　　　イ. o-ver　　　ウ. suc-ceed　　エ. ze-bra

C Complete the following English sentences to match the Japanese.【語彙と表現の知識】

(各3点)

1. 地球温暖化は深刻な問題です。

Global warming is a (　　　　　　) problem.

2. 私は自分のスキルを上げるために努力をします。

I will (　　　　　) an (　　　　　　) to improve my skills.

3. 私たちはお互いを尊敬する必要があります。

We need to (　　　　　) each other.

D Arrange the words in the proper order to match the Japanese.【表現と文法の知識・技能】

(各3点)

1. あなたのおかげでこの宿題を終えることができました。

(able / finish / I / thanks / to / to / was / you,) this homework.

_____

2. 彼はレースに勝ちそうだ。

He (is / likely / the race / to / win).

_____

3. 1992年に建てられたあの建物は建て替えられる予定です。

(built / in 1992, / is / the building, / was / which) going to be rebuilt.

_____

E Read the following passage and answer the questions below.

　　Japan, which has taken in a lot of foreign workers, is getting some benefits thanks to them. Nowadays, Japan's labor shortage is a critical problem. People from abroad have become an important workforce. (1)They will bring new ideas and build good atmospheres into workplaces in Japan.

　　There is another benefit. Some Japanese companies which employ foreign workers make English an official language (2) work. The workers can share a wider variety of ideas. As a result, (3)(are / likely / more / succeed / such companies / to) on the global stage.

　　In order to make our society more open to the world, we need to make an effort to understand various ways of thinking and respect different senses of values. If we do this, Japan will start a new chapter (4) we can all live better lives together.

1. 下線部(1)は何を指していますか。英語で答えなさい。【内容についての思考力・判断力・表現力】（3点）

....

2. 空所(2)に入る最も適当な語を選びなさい。【表現の知識】　　　　　　　　　　（3点）
　　ア．at　　　　　　　イ．in　　　　　　　ウ．on　　　　　　　エ．with

3. 下線部(3)の(　　)内の語句を適切に並べかえなさい。【表現の知識】　　　　　（3点）

....

4. 空所(4)に入る最も適当な語句を選びなさい。【表現の知識】　　　　　　　　　（3点）
　　ア．because of　　　イ．due to　　　　　ウ．seem to　　　　　エ．so that

5. 次の問いに英語で答えなさい。【内容についての思考力・判断力・表現力】　　　（各4点）
　　(1) What benefits will foreign workers bring to workplaces in Japan?

....

　　(2) Why do we need to make an effort to understand various ways of thinking and respect different senses of values?

....

True Love between a Cat and a Dog   Part 1

/50

A Translate the English into Japanese and the Japanese into English.【語彙の知識】(各1点)

1. kitten 名 B1 [   ]   2. bond 名 B1 [   ]

3. _____ 形 B1 忠実な   4. _____ 動 A2 …の価値を認める

5. independent 形 B1 [   ]   6. _____ 動 B2 …を愛する

B Choose the word whose underlined part is pronounced differently from the other three.【発音の知識】(各2点)

1. ア. bond   イ. come   ウ. love   エ. other

2. ア. appreciate   イ. feline   ウ. female   エ. independent

3. ア. kitten   イ. lives (life の複数形)   ウ. online   エ. while

C Complete the following English sentences to match the Japanese.【表現と文法の知識】

(各3点)

1. 妹は3年間その猫の世話をした。

   My sister (   ) (   ) the cat for three years.

2. 自分で物事を決めるのは私には難しい。

   It is difficult for me to decide things on (   ) (   ).

3. 私は昨日駅で見知らぬ人に話しかけられた。

   I was (   ) (   ) by a stranger at the station yesterday.

D Arrange the words in the proper order to match the Japanese.【表現と文法の知識・技能】

(各3点)

1. 友人や家族には誠実であるべきだ。

   You (be / loyal / should / to) your friends and family.

2. あなたがこのおもちゃで遊んだの？ 拾ってその箱に入れておいてね。

   Did you play with these toys? (and / pick / them / up) put them in the box.

3. そんなことをしたら他の人に笑われてしまうだろう。

   If you do such a thing, you will (at / be / by / laughed) others.

E Read the following passage and answer the questions below.

Our Recommended Book for This Month: *Coo and Shino*

On November 7, 2012, the kitten (1)(and / picked / taken / up / was) home by Haru-san. She named him Coo. Haru-san also looked (2) an old female dog, Shino. When Coo and Shino saw each other for the first time, Coo (3)(fall / in / love / seemed / to) with her. This was just the beginning of their story. Read a review from one of our readers.

David
A special bond between a feline (4)(name) Coo and his best canine friend, Shino Cats and dogs are people's favorite pet animals. Some people love dogs because they are loyal to their owners, while others appreciate that cats love (5)(live) independent lives on their own. Well, after you read this book, you may come to adore both cats and dogs!

---

1. 下線部(1), (3)の(　　)内の語を適切に並べかえなさい。【表現と文法の知識】　　　(各3点)

  (1) ....

  (3) ....

2. 空所(2)に入る最も適当な語を選びなさい。【表現の知識】　　　(2点)

  ア. after　　　　　イ. around　　　　ウ. before　　　　エ. by

3. 下線部(4), (5)の語を適切な形に変えなさい。【表現と文法の知識】　　　(各2点)

  (4) ....

  (5) ....

4. 次の問いに英語で答えなさい。【内容についての思考力・判断力・表現力】　　　(各4点)

  (1) How was Coo when he saw Shino for the first time?

  ....

  (2) Why do some people like dogs?

  ....

True Love between a Cat and a Dog   Part 2

/50

A Translate the English into Japanese and the Japanese into English.【語彙の知識】(各1点)

1. recall 動 B1 [   ]   2. ＿＿＿＿＿ 形 B1 相互の

3. ＿＿＿＿＿ 名 かくれんぼ   4. neighborhood 名 B1 [   ]

5. bump 動 B1 [   ]   6. ＿＿＿＿＿ 形 B2 穏やかな

B Choose the word whose underlined part is pronounced differently from the other three.【発音の知識】   (各2点)

1. ア. everything   イ. gently   ウ. stretch   エ. serene

2. ア. bump   イ. mutual   ウ. trust   エ. under

3. ア. eight   イ. neighbor   ウ. receive   エ. weight

C Complete the following English sentences to match the Japanese.【表現の知識】(各3点)

1. 私は昨日，担任の先生に偶然出くわした。

   I (   ) (   ) my homeroom teacher yesterday.

2. 彼女はクラス全員の注目を集めた。

   She (   ) (   ) from all her classmates.

3. ティミーは誰も見ていないときにお菓子に手を伸ばした。

   Timmy (   ) (   ) his hand to the candy while no one was watching him.

D Arrange the words in the proper order to match the Japanese.【表現と文法の知識・技能】

(各3点)

1. この部屋は会議で使用中です。

   This room (being / for / is / used) a meeting.

   ＿＿＿＿＿＿＿＿＿＿＿＿＿＿＿＿＿＿＿＿＿＿＿＿＿

2. 1日2回犬の散歩をします。

   I (dog / for / my / take) a walk twice a day.

   ＿＿＿＿＿＿＿＿＿＿＿＿＿＿＿＿＿＿＿＿＿＿＿＿＿

3. 好きなテレビドラマを見て週末を過ごすつもりです。

   I am going (spend / the weekend / to / watching) my favorite TV dramas.

   ＿＿＿＿＿＿＿＿＿＿＿＿＿＿＿＿＿＿＿＿＿＿＿＿＿

E Read the following passage and answer the questions below.

I tried everything to attract Shino's attention. Softly and gently, I stretched out my paw to her. (1) I touched her, however, Shino stood up and left me all alone. Still, I never (2)(give) up.

Day after day, I stayed beside Shino and followed her to every corner of Haru-san's home. Then, one day, Shino reached out her paw, and I softly touched it. Finally, mutual trust (3)(being / between / built / us / was).

Shino often (4)(spend) the day sitting in the sun near the window. We sometimes played hide-and-seek under a *kotatsu*. Every day, Haru-san took us for walks in the neighborhood. When we bumped into another dog we knew, we got excited.

It seemed like serene and happy (5)(days / last / like / this / would) forever.

1. 空所(1)に入る最も適当な語句を選びなさい。【表現の知識】　　　　　　　　　（2点）

　　ア. As far as　　　イ. As long as　　　ウ. As much as　　　エ. As soon as

2. 下線部(2), (4)の語を適切な形に変えなさい。【表現と文法の知識】　　　　　　　（各2点）

　　(2) _____

　　(4) _____

3. 下線部(3), (5)の(　　)内の語を適切に並べかえなさい。【表現と文法の知識】　　（各3点）

　　(3) _____

　　(5) _____

4. 次の問いに英語で答えなさい。【内容についての思考力・判断力・表現力】　　　（各4点）

　　(1) Why did Coo touch Shino, stay beside her, and follow her around?

　　_____

　　(2) When Coo and Shino bumped into another dog they knew, how did they feel?

　　_____

A Translate the English into Japanese and the Japanese into English.【語彙の知識】(各1点)

1. diagnose 動 [   ]   2. _____ 名   認知症

3. bark 動 B2 [   ]   4. _____ 副 B1   激しく

5. _____ 名   獣医   6. hospitalize 動 B2 [   ]

B Choose the word which has primary stress on a different syllable from the other three.【アクセントの知識】(各2点)

1. ア. de-spite   イ. gen-tly   ウ. near-by   エ. re-call

2. ア. be-gin-ning   イ. de-men-tia   ウ. di-ag-nose   エ. how-ev-er

3. ア. com-fort-a-ble   イ. hos-pi-tal-ize   ウ. in-de-pend-ent   エ. vi-o-lent-ly

C Complete the following English sentences to match the Japanese.【表現の知識】(各3点)

1. 東京駅はとても大きいから迷いやすいよ。

Tokyo Station is very big, so it is easy to (   ) (   ).

2. 何かが喉に詰まったようです。

It seems like I (   ) (   ) (   ) in my throat.

3. 両親が2日前にインフルエンザと診断されました。

My parents (   ) (   ) (   ) the flu two days ago.

D Arrange the words in the proper order to match the Japanese.【表現と文法の知識・技能】

(各3点)

1. ずっと具合が悪かったから，まったく楽しくなかった。

It (all / at / fun / not / was) because I felt sick all the time.

_____

2. ここが私が初めて彼女に出会った場所です。

This is (first / I / met / the place / where) her.

_____

3. 私たちの願いが叶う日が来ることを願っています。

I hope (come / that / the day / when / will) our wishes will come true.

_____

E Read the following passage and answer the questions below.

Then, one day in 2014, Shino began to walk straight into walls and even got herself stuck in small spaces. Soon, she started to circle around the same place again and again. Later, Shino was diagnosed with dementia.

I decided (1)(could / do / everything / I / to) for Shino. When she got lost, I served (2) her guide. Shino seemed to feel comfortable when she placed her head on my back. (3) all these efforts, however, in the summer of 2017, Shino couldn't stand up at all.

One night, Shino started to bark out violently. I didn't (4)(know / she / the reason / was / why) howling so hard. Early the next morning, Shino was (5)(take) to a veterinarian nearby and was hospitalized.

1. 下線部(1), (4)の(　　)内の語句を適切に並べかえなさい。【表現と文法の知識】　　（各3点）

   (1) ....

   (4) ....

2. 空所(2), (3)に入る最も適当な語を選びなさい。【語彙と表現の知識】　　（各2点）

   (2) ア. as　　　　　イ. for　　　　　ウ. to　　　　　エ. with

   (3) ア. Although　　イ. Despite　　　ウ. Instead　　　エ. Without

3. 下線部(5)の語を適切な形に変えなさい。【語彙と文法の知識】　　（2点）

   ....

4. 次の問いに英語で答えなさい。【内容についての思考力・判断力・表現力】　　（各4点）

   (1) Why did Shino walk straight into walls or circle around the same place again and again?

   ....

   (2) How did Shino look when she placed her head on Coo's back?

   ....

A Translate the English into Japanese and the Japanese into English.【語彙の知識】(各1点)

1. revive 動 B2 [   ] 2. approximately 副 B1 [   ]

3. _____ 動 …を元気づける 4. _____ 動 …を抱きしめる

5. _____ 名 B1 食欲 6. sorrow 名 B1 [   ]

B Choose the word whose underlined part is pronounced differently from the other three.【発音の知識】

(各2点)

1. ア. att<u>e</u>mpt イ. <u>e</u>ven ウ. l<u>e</u>ssen エ. v<u>e</u>t

2. ア. appr<u>o</u>ximately イ. bl<u>o</u>ssom ウ. c<u>o</u>mfort エ. h<u>o</u>spital

3. ア. <u>a</u>ppetite イ. <u>a</u>ttract ウ. embr<u>a</u>ce エ. gr<u>a</u>dually

C Complete the following English sentences to match the Japanese.【表現の知識】(各3点)

1. 彼は近いうちに亡くなるかもしれない。

He may (   ) (   ) soon.

2. 騒がしい子供たちのせいで落ち着いて本が読めない。

I cannot read a book (   ) (   ) because of the noisy children.

3. 私がアイロンがけをしている間，子供たちを見ていてくれますか。

Can you (   ) (   ) the kids while I do the ironing?

D Arrange the words in the proper order to match the Japanese.【表現と文法の知識・技能】

(各3点)

1. 桜が満開のときにまたここに来ようね。

Let's come here again when the cherry (are / bloom / blossoms / full / in).

_____

2. 2015年に私はここで働き始めたのだが，そのとき妻に出会った。

I started to work here (I / in 2015, / met / when) my wife.

_____

3. 私は福岡の故郷に帰省し，そこで3日間過ごした。

I went back to my hometown (Fukuoka, / I / in / stayed / where) for three days.

_____

E Read the following passage and answer the questions below.

At 2:30 p.m. on the day (1) Shino was hospitalized, there was a call from the hospital, and the vet said, "Shino-chan's heart has stopped." When Haru-san arrived at the hospital, the doctor was still (2)(attempt) to revive Shino. After approximately ten minutes, Haru-san said to the vet, "That is enough. Shino has comforted us so much." Shino finally stopped breathing in peace.

After Shino left us, Haru-san talked to me gently and embraced me warmly. But I (3)(like / didn't / talking / feel / to) anybody. I didn't even have an appetite.

(4)(as / by / time / went), however, my sorrow gradually lessened. I came to think that Shino would always watch over us with her gentle eyes. In our yard, where Shino and I (5) so much time together, the cherry blossoms were in full bloom.

1. 空所(1)に入る最も適当な語を選びなさい。【文法の知識】 （2点）

　ア. how　　　　　イ. what　　　　　ウ. when　　　　エ. which

2. 下線部(2)の語を適切な形に変えなさい。【表現と文法の知識】 （2点）

　　...

3. 下線部(3), (4)の(　)内の語を適切に並べかえなさい。【表現の知識】 （各3点）

　　(3) ....

　　(4) ....

4. 空所(5)に入る最も適当な語(句)を選びなさい。【文法の知識】 （2点）

　　ア. had spent　　　イ. have spent　　　ウ. spend　　　エ. was spent

5. 次の問いに英語で答えなさい。【内容についての思考力・判断力・表現力】 （各4点）

　　(1) In what way did Shino stop breathing?

　　...

　　(2) What did Coo come to think as his sorrow gradually lessened?

　　...

The Joker

Part 1

/50

A Translate the English into Japanese and the Japanese into English. 【語彙の知識】（各1点）

1. _____ 名 B1 葬式　　　　2. occasion 名 B1　　[　　　　　]

3. relative 名 B1　　[　　　　　]　　4. pour 動 A2　　[　　　　　]

5. superior 形 B1　　[　　　　　]　　6. _____ 動 B2 うなずく

B Choose the word whose underlined part is pronounced differently from the other three. 【発音の知識】

(各2点)

1. ア. c<u>oa</u>t　　　イ. c<u>o</u>ffin　　　ウ. m<u>o</u>ment　　　エ. sh<u>o</u>ne

2. ア. f<u>a</u>vorite　　イ. im<u>a</u>gine　　ウ. str<u>ai</u>ght　　エ. t<u>a</u>ste

3. ア. e<u>x</u>amine　　イ. e<u>x</u>hausted　　ウ. e<u>x</u>hibition　　エ. e<u>x</u>ist

C Complete the following English sentences to match the Japanese. 【表現の知識】　（各3点）

1. 彼はまるで「そんなドレスは買うな」と言わんばかりに首を振った。

He shook his head (　　　　　) (　　　　　) to say "don't buy such a dress."

2. 湖の周りを車でまわる代わりに船に乗ることもできます。

You can take the boat (　　　　　) (　　　　　) driving around the lake.

3. 彼が本気のはずがない。ただあなたをからかっているだけですよ。

He can't be serious. He is just (　　　　　) your (　　　　　).

D Arrange the words in the proper order to match the Japanese. 【表現と文法の知識・技能】

(各3点)

1. 赤ちゃんはあおむけになっていました。

(its / lying / on / the baby / was) back.

2. あなたがスーツを着ているのを見るのは初めてね。

(a suit / have / I / in / never / seen / you) before.

3. 気分が悪い。あんなにチョコレートを食べなければよかった。

I feel sick. I (eaten / have / much / shouldn't / so) chocolate.

E Read the following passage and answer the questions below.

It was a very happy funeral, a great success. Even the sun shone that day for the late Henry Ground. Lying in his coffin, he was probably enjoying himself too. Once more, and for the last time on this earth, he was the center of attention. Yes, it was a very happy occasion. People laughed and told each other jokes. Relatives who (1) not spoken for years smiled at each other and promised to stay in touch. And, of course, everyone had a favorite story to tell about Henry.

"Do you remember the time he dressed up (2) very strange clothes and went from door to door telling people's fortunes? He actually made six pounds in an afternoon!"

"I was once having dinner with him in a restaurant. When the wine waiter brought the wine, he poured a drop into Henry's glass and waited with a superior expression on his face, as if to say 'Taste it. It's clear that you know *nothing* about wine.' So Henry, instead (3) tasting it the way any normal person would do, put his thumb and forefinger into the wine. Then he put his hand to his ear and rubbed his forefinger and thumb together as if he were *listening* to the quality of the wine! Then he nodded to the wine waiter seriously, as if to say 'Yes, that's fine. You may serve it.' You (4)(should see) the wine waiter's face! I still don't know how Henry managed to keep a straight face!"

"Old Henry loved to pull people's legs. Once, when he was invited to an exhibition of some modern painter's latest work, he managed somehow to get into the exhibition hall the day before and turn all the paintings upside down. The exhibition ran for four days before anyone noticed what he had done!"

"It's hard to believe that Henry was a Ground when you think how different he was from his brothers."

1. 空所(1), (2), (3)に入る最も適当な語を選びなさい。【文法と語彙の知識】　　　　　(各3点)

   (1) ア. did　　　イ. do　　　　ウ. had　　　　エ. have

   (2) ア. for　　　イ. in　　　　ウ. on　　　　エ. with

   (3) ア. by　　　イ. for　　　　ウ. of　　　　エ. with

2. 下線部(4)の語句を適切な形に変えなさい。【文法の知識】　　　　　(3点)

_____

3. 次の問いに英語で答えなさい。【内容についての思考力・判断力・表現力】　　　　　(各4点)

   (1) How did Henry make six pounds?

_____

   (2) What expression did the wine waiter give Henry when he poured him a glass of wine?

_____

The Joker

Part 2

/50

A Translate the English into Japanese and the Japanese into English. 【語彙の知識】 (各1点)

1. unimportant 形 A2　　[　　　　　　　] 2. ＿＿＿＿＿＿ 名 A2　弁護士

3. charming 形 B2　　[　　　　　　　] 4. ＿＿＿＿＿＿ 名 A2　疑い, 疑念

5. energetic 形 A2　　[　　　　　　　] 6. ＿＿＿＿＿＿ 名 B1　友達, 連れ

B Choose the word which has primary stress on a different syllable from the other three. 【アクセントの知識】　　(各2点)

1. ア. for-tune　　　イ. man-age　　　ウ. some-how　　　エ. suc-cess

2. ア. com-pan-ion　イ. fa-vor-ite　　ウ. fu-ner-al　　　エ. qual-i-ty

3. ア. ac-tiv-i-ty　　イ. di-am-e-ter　　ウ. en-er-get-ic　　エ. su-pe-ri-or

C Complete the following English sentences to match the Japanese. 【表現の知識】　(各3点)

1. メグは大家族に生まれた。

Meg was (　　　　　　) (　　　　　　) a large family.

2. 彼女は作家になりたいと思い続けていたが, 結局は教師になった。

She had always wanted to be a writer but ended (　　　　　　)
(　　　　　　) a teacher.

3. 今朝は雨になりそうだったが, いい天気になった。

Although it looked like rain this morning, it has (　　　　　　)
(　　　　　　) to be a fine day.

D Arrange the words in the proper order to match the Japanese. 【表現と文法の知識・技能】

(各3点)

1. 彼は事業を成功させようと実に努力した。

He really (a success / make / of / the business / to / tried).

＿＿＿＿＿＿＿＿＿＿＿＿＿＿＿＿＿＿＿＿＿＿＿＿＿＿＿＿＿

2. 私は朝食を食べませんでした。それで腹ぺこなのです。

I did not eat breakfast. (am / hungry / I / is / that / why).

＿＿＿＿＿＿＿＿＿＿＿＿＿＿＿＿＿＿＿＿＿＿＿＿＿＿＿＿＿

3. トムはジーンズをはいてパーティーにやって来た。それにはみんなびっくりした。

Tom came (everybody / in / jeans, / surprised / the party / to / which).

＿＿＿＿＿＿＿＿＿＿＿＿＿＿＿＿＿＿＿＿＿＿＿＿＿＿＿＿＿

E Read the following passage and answer the questions below.

Yes, it was difficult to believe that he was a Ground. He was born (1) an unimportant but well-to-do Midlands family. He was the youngest of five sons. The Grounds were all handsome: blue-eyed, fair-haired, clever and hardworking. The four older boys all (2)(a / lives / made / of / success / their). The eldest became a clergyman; the second ended (3) as the headmaster of a famous public school; the third went into business and became very rich; the fourth became a lawyer like his father. That is why everybody was surprised when the youngest Ground, Henry, turned out to be a good-for-nothing.

(4) his brothers, he had brown eyes and dark hair, but was as handsome and charming as the rest, which made him quite a lady-killer. And, although he never married, there is no doubt at all that Henry Ground loved women. He also loved eating, drinking, laughing, talking, and a thousand other activities which don't make money or improve the human condition. One of his favorite ways of spending time was doing nothing. His idea of an energetic afternoon when the sun was shining was to sit in the shade of a tree, with a pretty companion by his side, talking of this and that, counting the blades of grass, and learning the songs of the birds.

1. 空所(1), (3)に入る最も適当な語を選びなさい。【語彙の知識】　　　　　　　（各3点）

  (1) ア. above　　　　イ. into　　　　　ウ. to　　　　　エ. under

  (3) ア. in　　　　　イ. on　　　　　　ウ. up　　　　　エ. with

2. 下線部(2)の(　　)内の語を適切に並べかえなさい。【表現の知識】　　　　　　（3点）

_____

3. 空所(4)に入る最も適当な語を選びなさい。【語彙の知識】　　　　　　　　　　（3点）

  ア. Among　　　　イ. Beside　　　　ウ. Unlike　　　　エ. Without

4. 次の問いに英語で答えなさい。【内容についての思考力・判断力・表現力】　　　（各4点）

  (1) What kind of family was Henry born into?

_____

  (2) What was one of Henry's favorite ways of spending time?

_____

The Joker

Part 3

/50

A Translate the English into Japanese and the Japanese into English.【語彙の知識】（各1点）

1. invitation 名 B1　　[　　　　　　　]　　2. possibly 副 A2　　[　　　　　　　　]

3. _____ 動 B1　静まる，落ち着く　　4. _____ 形 A2　切望して

5. worth 形 B1　　[　　　　　　　]　　6. pause 動 B1　　[　　　　　　　　]

B Choose the word whose underlined part is pronounced differently from the other three.【発音の知識】　　　　　　（各2点）

1. ア. c<u>o</u>ffin　　イ. exh<u>au</u>sted　　ウ. p<u>au</u>se　　エ. thr<u>oa</u>t

2. ア. gr<u>a</u>ve　　イ. l<u>a</u>dy　　ウ. l<u>a</u>ter　　エ. r<u>ea</u>dy

3. ア. <u>th</u>eater　　イ. <u>th</u>eme　　ウ. smoo<u>th</u>　　エ. wor<u>th</u>

C Complete the following English sentences to match the Japanese.【表現の知識】　（各3点）

1. 会議は，私が思っていたよりもはるかに長く続いた。

The meeting (　　　　　　) (　　　　　　　) for a lot longer than I expected.

2. 少しの間落ち着いてくれませんか。

Would you just (　　　　　　) (　　　　　　) for a minute?

3. 私は生徒たち一人一人と順番に話をしました。

I spoke to each of the students (　　　　　　) (　　　　　).

D Arrange the words in the proper order to match the Japanese.【表現と文法の知識・技能】

（各3点）

1. 彼はまだ学生であった間に事業を始めました。

He (a business / at / he / school / started / still / was / while).

_____

2. 私は教会での結婚式に出席しました。

(at / attended / I / the church / the wedding).

_____

3. 私はその機械がどのようにして動くのか知りたいと思っていました。

I (about / curious / how / the machine / was / works).

_____

E Read the following passage and answer the questions below.

Anyway, the stories went on even while (1)(being / into / lowered / the coffin / the grave / was). People held handkerchiefs to their eyes, but their tears were tears of laughter, not sadness. Later, there was a funeral breakfast, by invitation only. It was attended by twelve of Henry's closest friends. Henry Ground had asked his brother, Colin, to read out his will during the funeral breakfast. Everyone was curious about Henry Ground's will. Henry had always been borrowing money from others, (2) he? What could he possibly have to leave in a will?

Colin cleared his throat. "Ahem! If you are ready, ladies and gentlemen." Everyone settled down, (3)anxious to know what was in the will. Colin opened the will. When he announced that Henry Ground was, in fact, worth at least three-quarters of a million pounds, everyone gasped. But who was going to get it? Eyes narrowed and throats went dry.

"You are all such dear friends of mine," Colin went on, "that I cannot decide which of you to leave my money to." Colin paused. In the silence, you could have heard a pin drop. He began to read the will again. "So, dear friends, I have set you a little competition. Each of you (4) must tell the funniest joke he or she can think of, and the one who gets the most laughter will get my fortune. Colin will be the only judge of the best joke."

1. 下線部(1)の（　　）内の語を適切に並べかえなさい。【表現と文法の知識】　　　　　（3点）

2. 空所(2)に入る最も適当な語を答えなさい。【表現と文法の知識】　　　　　　　　　（3点）
   （　　　　　　　）

3. 下線部(3)anxious の前に省略されている１語を答えなさい。【表現と文法の知識】　　（3点）
   （　　　　　　　）

4. 空所(4)に「順番に」の意味になる熟語を２語で答えなさい。【表現の知識】　　　　（3点）
   （　　　　　　　）（　　　　　　　）

5. 次の問いに英語で答えなさい。【内容についての思考力・判断力・表現力】　　　　　（各4点）

   (1) Who were invited to the funeral breakfast?

   (2) Who could get Henry's fortune according to his will?

The Joker

Part 4

/50

A Translate the English into Japanese and the Japanese into English.【語彙の知識】(各1点)

1. ＿＿＿＿＿＿＿ 動 A2 …を埋める，…を隠す
2. sneeze 動 B2 [　　　　　　　]
3. desperately 副 B2 [　　　　　　　]
4. ＿＿＿＿＿＿＿ 名 B1 欲求，欲望
5. ＿＿＿＿＿＿＿ 形 B1 できない
6. practical 形 B1 [　　　　　　　]

B Choose the word which has primary stress on a different syllable from the other three.【アクセントの知識】(各2点)

1. ア. de-sire　　　イ. nar-row　　　ウ. pre-tend　　　エ. un-like
2. ア. com-plete-ly　　イ. per-fect-ly　　ウ. un-a-ble　　エ. vol-ca-no
3. ア. com-pe-ti-tion　イ. des-per-ate-ly　ウ. or-di-nar-y　エ. se-ri-ous-ly

C Complete the following English sentences to match the Japanese.【表現の知識】(各3点)

1. 家族は彼の本当の死因を隠そうとした。

His family tried to (　　　　　) (　　　　　) the real cause of his death.

2. 私たちが劇場に着くまでに，劇はもう始まっていた。

(　　　　　) the (　　　　　) we got to the theater, the play had already started.

3. この薬を飲めば，すぐに気分がよくなりますよ。

Take this medicine and you'll be feeling better (　　　　　) (　　　　　) time.

D Arrange the words in the proper order to match the Japanese.【表現の知識・技能】(各3点)

1. 彼らはスペインでお互いに恋に落ちた。

They (each / fell / in / in / love / other / with) Spain.

＿＿＿＿＿＿＿＿＿＿＿＿＿＿＿＿＿＿＿＿＿＿＿＿＿＿＿＿＿＿＿＿

2. 子供は長い時間静かにしていることはできない。

(a / can't / children / for / long / quiet / remain / time).

＿＿＿＿＿＿＿＿＿＿＿＿＿＿＿＿＿＿＿＿＿＿＿＿＿＿＿＿＿＿＿＿

3. 家に着くころには，私たちは疲れて空腹だった。

(by / got / home / the time / we), we were tired and hungry.

＿＿＿＿＿＿＿＿＿＿＿＿＿＿＿＿＿＿＿＿＿＿＿＿＿＿＿＿＿＿＿＿

E Read the following passage and answer the questions below.

The first person stood up and told a very funny joke about an Englishman who fell in love with his umbrella. When he finished, he was in tears of laughter, for he always laughed at his own jokes. The rest of the company remained *completely silent*. You could tell from their red faces that they found the joke funny, but not one of them wanted to laugh, and give him the chance to win the competition. The second told a story about a hungry pig, which was so good that, some years later, a movie company paid for the story. When she sat down, the others buried their faces in their handkerchiefs, pretended to sneeze, dropped pencils under the table —— anything to cover up their laughter. And so it went (1), joke after wonderful joke, the sort of jokes that would make your sides ache. And yet, everybody somehow kept from (2)(laugh)!

By the time the last joke had been told, every one of the twelve was sitting perfectly still, desperately holding in the laughter which was bursting to get out. Their desire to laugh had built up such a pressure: (3)(a volcano / erupt / it / like / ready / to / was).

Silence. Painful silence.

Suddenly, Colin sneezed. A perfectly ordinary sneeze. Atishoo. Then he took out a ridiculously large handkerchief with red spots on it and blew his nose. Bbbrrrrrrppp.

That was enough. Someone burst out laughing, unable to hold it in any longer. That started the others off. In no time, everyone bent (4), tears running down their cheeks as they laughed. Of course, they were not just laughing at the sneeze, nor even at the twelve jokes. No, they were laughing at themselves as they realized that Henry Ground had led them into his last, and funniest, practical joke, setting their need to laugh against their greed for money.

1. 空所(1), (4)に入る最も適当な語を選びなさい。【表現の知識】　　　　　（各3点）

　(1) ア. by　　　　　イ. for　　　　　ウ. on　　　　　エ. to

　(4) ア. in　　　　　イ. over　　　　　ウ. to　　　　　エ. under

2. 下線部(2)の語を適切な形に変えなさい。【表現の知識】　　　　　　　　（3点）

3. 下線部(3)の(　　　)内の語を適切に並べかえなさい。【表現と文法の知識】　（3点）

4. 次の問いに英語で答えなさい。【内容についての思考力・判断力・表現力】　（各4点）

　(1) How could we tell that they found the first person's joke funny?

　(2) What were they really laughing at after Colin's sneeze?

The Joker

Part 5

/50

A Translate the English into Japanese and the Japanese into English.【語彙の知識】(各1点)

1. forgive 動 B1　　[　　　　　　　] 2. _____ 副　不必要に

3. overcome 動 B1　[　　　　　　　] 4. divide 動 A2　　[　　　　　　　]

5. _____ 副 B1　等しく，平等に 6. _____ 接 B1　～するときはいつでも

B Choose the word whose underlined part is pronounced differently from the other three.【発音の知識】

(各2点)

1. ア. bl<u>ow</u>　　　イ. j<u>o</u>ke　　　ウ. p<u>au</u>se　　　エ. thr<u>oa</u>t

2. ア. div<u>i</u>de　　イ. f<u>i</u>nal　　　ウ. s<u>i</u>lent　　　エ. tw<u>i</u>nkle

3. ア. <u>h</u>andkerchief　イ. <u>h</u>onor　ウ. laug<u>h</u>ter　エ. neig<u>h</u>bor

C Complete the following English sentences to match the Japanese.【表現の知識】(各3点)

1. 嵐はついにおさまって，あたりは静かになった。

The storm (　　　　　　) (　　　　　　) at last and all was quiet.

2. テレビの映像を見て，その危険が私にも切実に感じられました。

The danger really came (　　　　　) (　　　　　) me when I saw the pictures on TV.

3. トムは部屋にいます。スティーヴについては，どこにいるか私は知りません。

Tom is in his room. (　　　　　) (　　　　　) Steve, I have no idea where he is.

D Arrange the words in the proper order to match the Japanese.【表現と文法の知識・技能】

(各3点)

1. 彼女は目を輝かせて，その話をした。

She (her eyes / the story / told / twinkling / with).

_____

2. ステファンは，新しい先生にいたずらをすることにした。

Stephan (a joke / decided / his / new teacher / on / play / to).

_____

3. 死後，彼のお金は3人の子供たちの間で分けられた。

After his death, (among / children / divided / his / his money / three / was).

_____

E Read the following passage and answer the questions below.

When, at long last, the laughter had died down, Colin cleared his throat once more. "Forgive my little piece of theater," he said, his eyes twinkling. "I have been practicing that sneeze for a week or more." He folded the large handkerchief and put it back into his pocket. "Henry's idea, of course," he added, unnecessarily. All twelve guests realized they had been set up beautifully.

"Ahem! May I read you the rest of the will now?" Colin asked.

"My friends," the last part of Henry's will began, "forgive me, but I couldn't help (1)(play) one last little joke on you. It's good to know that your love of laughter finally overcame your love of money."

Colin paused, letting (2)(come / home / of / the meaning / the words / to) everybody. Then he read out the final part of the late Henry Ground's last will.

"My friends, thank you for letting me have the last laugh. As (3) the money: because I love you all, my fortune will be divided equally (4) you. Enjoy your share, and think of me whenever you hear laughter."

The company fell silent. For the first time that day, there was a feeling of sadness in the air.

1. 下線部(1)の語を適切な形に変えなさい。【表現と文法の知識】　　　　　　　　（3点）

2. 下線部(2)の（　　）内の語を適切に並べかえなさい。【表現と文法の知識】　　（3点）

3. 空所(3), (4)に入る最も適当な語を選びなさい。【語彙と表現の知識】　　　（各3点）
   (3) ア. for　　　　　イ. if　　　　　ウ. of　　　　　エ. on
   (4) ア. among　　　イ. between　　　ウ. into　　　　エ. under

4. 次の問いに英語で答えなさい。【内容についての思考力・判断力・表現力】　　（各4点）
   (1) What did the twelve guests realize after the laughter?

   (2) What did Henry's will say it was good to know?

A Translate the English into Japanese and the Japanese into English.【語彙の知識】（各1点）

1. _____ 名 　　ドローン
2. _____ 動 B1 　…を得点する
3. _____ 名 B1 　直径
4. extremely 副 A2 　　[　　　　　　　]
5. entertainment 名 A2 　[　　　　　　]
6. enjoyable 形 B1 　　[　　　　　　　]

B Choose the word which has primary stress on a different syllable from the other three.【アクセントの知識】 （各2点）

1. ア. dif-fi-cult　　イ. ex-treme-ly　　ウ. fes-ti-val　　エ. med-i-cine
2. ア. com-put-er　　イ. ex-cel-lent　　ウ. fam-i-ly　　エ. stu-di-o
3. ア. en-joy-a-ble　イ. en-ter-tain-ment　ウ. par-tic-i-pate　エ. tech-nol-o-gy

C Complete the following English sentences to match the Japanese.【表現と文法の知識】

（各3点）

1. 私はキュウリではなくトマトが好きです。

　I (　　　　　　) tomatoes, (　　　　　　) cucumbers.

2. 大雪のために彼は遅れました。

　He was (　　　　　) (　　　　　) it snowed a lot.

3. 由紀の息子の身長が192センチと聞いて私は驚きました。

　I was (　　　　　) (　　　　　) I heard Yuki's son was 192 centimeters

　tall.

D Arrange the words in the proper order to match the Japanese.【表現と文法の知識・技能】

（各3点）

1. 車を運転することは自転車に乗るよりも難しい。

　(a bike / a car / difficult / driving / is / more / riding / than).

_____

2. そのタイヤは直径85センチです。

　(diameter / in / is / the tire / 85 centimeters).

_____

3. 朝から頭痛がひどかったので，彼女は仕事に行かなかった。

　She didn't go to work (a / bad / because / had / headache / she) in the

　morning.

_____

E Read the following passage and answer the questions below.

Vivian: Hey, what are you watching?

Takashi: I'm watching soccer!

Vivian: That's soccer? Those look like drones, not soccer balls!

Takashi: That's right. Five players on each team are trying to score goals (1) drones. A goal is scored when a drone goes through the ring. The team with more points wins.

Vivian: Playing drone soccer looks more difficult than playing soccer on a field!

Takashi: It really is. Players need excellent skills because the ring is only 55 centimeters in diameter.

Vivian: I see. Oh, the players (2)(be) flying the drones at extremely high speeds!

Takashi: Right. I (3)(see) a news story about a drone race the other day. I was surprised that an eleven-year-old boy won the race!

Vivian: (4)

Takashi: (5)New technologies are creating new forms of entertainment and making them more enjoy.

1. 空所(1)を含む文が「それぞれチームで5人の選手がドローンで得点しようとしている」という意味になるように，空所に入る最も適当な語を選びなさい。【語彙の知識】 （2点）

　　ア. at 　　　　　　イ. in 　　　　　　ウ. on 　　　　　　エ. with

2. 下線部(2), (3)の語を適切な形に変えなさい。【文法の知識】 （各3点）

　　(2) _____

　　(3) _____

3. 空所(4)に入る最も適当な表現を選びなさい。【表現の知識】 （2点）

　　ア. Fantastic! 　　　イ. I'm happy! 　　　ウ. No way! 　　　エ. That's too bad!

4. 下線部(5)には文法的な誤りが1箇所あります。誤りを指摘して正しなさい。【文法の知識】 （2点）

　　誤) _____ → 正) _____

5. 次の問いに英語で答えなさい。【内容についての思考力・判断力・表現力】 （各4点）

　　(1) Which looks more difficult to Vivian, playing soccer with drones or playing on a field?

　　　　_____

　　(2) Why do players need excellent skills?

　　_____

A Society with Drones

Part 2

/50

A Translate the English into Japanese and the Japanese into English. 【語彙の知識】 (各1点)

1. _____ 形 A2　軍の，軍用の
2. _____ 副 A2　最近，近頃
3. _____ 副 A2　あいにく，残念ながら
4. invade 動 A2　[　　　　　]
5. resolution 名 B2　[　　　　　]
6. unexpectedly 副 B1　[　　　　　]

B Choose the word which has primary stress on a different syllable from the other three. 【アクセントの知識】 (各2点)

1. ア. at-ten-tion　　イ. fac-to-ry　　ウ. in-ter-est　　エ. pri-va-cy
2. ア. ar-ti-cle　　イ. cam-er-a　　ウ. fa-vor-ite　　エ. vol-un-teer
3. ア. ac-ci-dent　　イ. mem-o-ry　　ウ. mu-se-um　　エ. u-ni-form

C Complete the following English sentences to match the Japanese. 【表現と文法の知識】

(各3点)

1. その公園にはたくさんの子供たちがいます。

   (　　　　　) are many children (　　　　　) the park.
2. 慶子は海水浴を楽しんでいます。

   Keiko is (　　　　　) (　　　　　) in the sea.
3. その問題を解決するのは難しいかもしれません。

   It (　　　　　) (　　　　　) difficult (　　　　　) solve the problem.

D Arrange the words in the proper order to match the Japanese. 【表現と文法の知識・技能】

(各3点)

1. 孝は病院へ運ばれたので，今，ここにはいません。

   Takashi (been / has / taken / the hospital / to), so he is not here now.

   _____

2. 私は健也に嘘をつかれたことがあります。

   I (a lie / been / before / by / have / told / Kenya).

   _____

3. 典子は椅子に座って本を読んでいます。

   (the chair, / is / Noriko / sitting / reading / on / a book).

   _____

E Read the following passage and answer the questions below.

Drones have been used (1) different purposes (2) many years. More than 70 years ago, they were developed for military purposes. Recently, people have found many other uses for these unmanned aerial vehicles.

Unfortunately, however, (3)(are / drones / problems / some / there / with). First, some people are against them because they might invade personal privacy. Today more people can enjoy flying drones than before. Drones with high resolution cameras fly (4)(take) pictures from above. We don't know when secret cameras are taking shots of us, and it may be very difficult to protect people's privacy.

Second, drones can have accidents even when they are flying in good weather. These aerial vehicles might unexpectedly fall from the sky, and (5)this can hurt people walking on the street.

1. 空所(1), (2)に入る最も適当な語を答えなさい。【文法の知識】　　　　　　(各2点)

　　(1) (　　　　　　　)

　　(2) (　　　　　　　)

2. 下線部(3)の(　　　)内の語を適切に並べかえなさい。【表現と文法の知識】　　　(3点)

3. 下線部(4)の語を適切な形に変えなさい。【文法の知識】　　　　　　　　　　(2点)

4. 下線部(5)は何を指していますか。日本語で答えなさい。【内容についての思考力・判断力・表現力】

　　　　　　　　　　　　　　　　　　　　　　　　　　　　　　　　　　　(3点)

5. 次の問いに英語で答えなさい。【内容についての思考力・判断力・表現力】　　(各4点)

　　(1) What was the purpose of developing drones more than 70 years ago?

　　(2) Can drones have accidents even when they are flying in good weather?

A Translate the English into Japanese and the Japanese into English.【語彙の知識】（各1点）

1. _____ 名 肥料　　　　　2. _____ 名 殺虫剤

3. _____ 名 B1 削減　　　　4. survivor 名 B1　　[　　　　　]

5. contaminate 動 B2　[　　　・　　]　6. radiation 名 B1　[　　　　　]

B Choose the word which has primary stress on a different syllable from the other three.【アクセントの知識】　　　　　　　　　　　　　　　　（各2点）

1. ア. ag-ri-cul-ture　　イ. ed-u-ca-tion　　ウ. il-lus-tra-tion　　エ. sit-u-a-tion

2. ア. choc-o-late　　イ. o-pin-ion　　ウ. pest-i-cide　　エ. ra-di-o

3. ア. di-a-ry　　イ. dif-fer-ence　　ウ. dis-as-ter　　エ. in-flu-ence

C Complete the following English sentences to match the Japanese.【表現と文法の知識】

（各3点）

1. 私は野球を見るのが好きです。野球をするのもまた好きです。

　I like watching baseball.　I like playing baseball (　　　　　　)
　(　　　　　　).

2. 私の息子はみんな，家族経営のビジネスに貢献している。

　All of my sons (　　　　　　) (　　　　　　) the family business.

3. 携帯電話は私たちの生活をより便利にしてくれる。

　Cell phones (　　　　　　) our lives (　　　　　　) convenient.

D Arrange the words in the proper order to match the Japanese.【表現と文法の知識・技能】

（各3点）

1. このアイデアはより多くの雇用創出に役立つだろう。

　(create / help / jobs / more / this idea / to / will).

2. 鳥が私の頭上を飛び越えていったことに気づかなかった。

　I didn't (flew / my head / notice / over / that / the bird).

3. 私は病気だったので，友人に会議を代わってもらいました。

　(me / my friend / of / place / the / took) at the meeting because I was ill.

E Read the following passage and answer the questions below.

Drones have brought many benefits to us as well. In agriculture, (1), farmers can sow seeds and spread fertilizer and pesticides on fields by using drones. This can be a great help especially for older farmers. Drones may help to solve labor shortages and may contribute to shorter working hours, cost reductions, and improved safety.

Also, drones can find survivors after disasters. Rescue workers sometimes cannot scramble in (2)(p   ) of debris or reach disaster areas (3)(contaminate) by radiation. However, drones can fly over such dangerous areas.

Drones, (4), make our entertainment more enjoyable. They are used in many concerts and sporting events for better camera and lighting angles. (5)Drones might even take the place of traditional fireworks shows in the future.

1. 空所(1), (4)に入る最も適当な語(句)をそれぞれ選びなさい。【表現の知識】　（各2点）

ア. because of　　イ. for example　　ウ. furthermore　　エ. however

(1) (　　　)　　(4) (　　　)

2. 下線部(2)が「山のような」という意味になるように，空所に入る最も適当な語を答えなさい。ただし，与えられた文字で始めること。【表現と語彙の知識】　（2点）

p＿＿＿＿＿＿＿＿＿＿　of

3. 下線部(3)の語を適切な形に変えなさい。【文法の知識】　（3点）

＿＿＿＿＿＿＿＿＿＿＿＿＿

4. 下線部(5)を日本語にしなさい。【表現と文法の知識】　（3点）

＿＿＿＿＿＿＿＿＿＿＿＿＿

5. 次の問いに英語で答えなさい。【内容についての思考力・判断力・表現力】　（各4点）

(1) What may drones help to solve?

＿＿＿＿＿＿＿＿＿＿＿＿＿

(2) For what are drones used in many concerts and sporting events?

＿＿＿＿＿＿＿＿＿＿＿＿＿

A Society with Drones

A Translate the English into Japanese and the Japanese into English. 【語彙の知識】(各1点)

1. ＿＿＿＿＿＿ 動 B1　…を配達する　　2. ＿＿＿＿＿＿ 副　効率的に

3. ＿＿＿＿＿＿ 形 B2　感染性の　　4. pandemic 名　[　　　　　]

5. viral 形　[　　　　　]　　6. inspect 動 B2　[　　　　　]

B Choose the word which has primary stress on a different syllable from the other three. 【アクセントの知識】(各2点)

1. ア. fam-i-ly　　イ. in-fec-tious　　ウ. pi-an-o　　エ. pro-duc-er

2. ア. a-gain　　イ. meth-od　　ウ. mu-sic　　エ. sun-shine

3. ア. de-liv-er　　イ. in-fec-tious　　ウ. pan-dem-ic　　エ. prom-is-ing

C Complete the following English sentences to match the Japanese. 【表現と文法の知識】

(各3点)

1. 裕二郎はさよならを言わずに部屋を出た。

   Yujiro left the room (　　　　　　) saying good-bye.

2. かつては福岡から熊本まで電車で1時間以上かかった。

   It took more than one hour from Fukuoka to Kumamoto by train (　　　　　) the (　　　　　).

3. このグループの将来に注目してください。

   Please (　　　　　) your (　　　　　) on the future of this group.

D Arrange the words in the proper order to match the Japanese. 【表現と文法の知識・技能】

(各3点)

1. 茜は昨日忙しかったに違いない。

   Akane (been / busy / have / must / yesterday).

2. あなたは辞書を上手く使うべきです。

   You (good / make / of / should / the dictionary / use).

3. 古いものは売り切れていたので，別の商品を買わないといけません。

   I (another / buy / have / product / since / to) the old one was sold out.

E Read the following passage and answer the questions below.

In our society of the future, delivery companies will use drones to deliver products more quickly and efficiently. Delivery drones may help people a lot if they have to stay home (1) an infectious disease pandemic. They may be one of the safest delivery methods that can be used without (2)(spread) viral infections.

Drones will do other jobs, too. Construction companies will use drones to inspect buildings and bridges efficiently. Since Japan's infrastructure is aging, (3)(by / drones / inspections / prompt / using / very useful / will be). Security companies will make use of drones as "bodyguards" in the sky.

Many people may have had negative feelings toward these flying vehicles in the past. However, the future of drones will certainly be promising and exciting. (4) your eyes on further drone developments!

1. 空所(1)に入る最も適当な語を選びなさい。【文法の知識】　　　　　　　　　　（3点）

　　ア. during　　　　　イ. when　　　　　ウ. while

2. 下線部(2)の語を適切な形に変えなさい。【文法の知識】　　　　　　　　　　　（3点）

　　..

3. 下線部(3)の(　　)内の語句を適切に並べかえなさい。【表現と文法の知識】　　（3点）

　　..

4. 空所(4)を含む文が「今後のドローンの進化に注目しよう！」という意味になるように，空所に入る最も適当な語を選びなさい。【表現の知識】　　　　　　　　　　　　　　（3点）

　　ア. Close　　　　　イ. Keep　　　　　ウ. Look　　　　　エ. Watch

5. 次の問いに英語で答えなさい。【内容についての思考力・判断力・表現力】　　　（各4点）

　　(1) Why will delivery companies use drones in the future?

　　..

　　(2) How will security companies make use of drones?

　　..

"Cloning" Cultural Properties

Part 1

/50

A Translate the English into Japanese and the Japanese into English.【語彙の知識】(各1点)

1. _____ 名　チラシ, ビラ　　　2. property 名 B1　[　　　　　　]

3. insight 名 B1　[　　　　　]　　　4. _____ 名　芸術作品

5. _____ 前 A2　…を除いて　　　6. discount 名 B1　[　　　　　]

B Choose the word which has primary stress on a different syllable from the other three.【アクセントの知識】(各2点)

1. ア. art-work　　イ. dis-count　　ウ. ex-cept　　エ. in-sight

2. ア. base-ment　　イ. be-fore　　ウ. fly-er　　エ. sen-ior

3. ア. ad-mis-sion　　イ. gen-er-al　　ウ. hol-i-day　　エ. prop-er-ty

C Complete the following English sentences to match the Japanese.【表現の知識】(各3点)

1. 昼ごはんを一緒に食べませんか。

Why (　　　　　) (　　　　　　　　　) have lunch together?

2. それらは無料で利用できます。

They (　　　　　) (　　　　　　　　　) for free.

3. 詳しくは104ページを参照すること。

(　　　　　) (　　　　　　　　　) information, see page 104.

D Arrange the words in the proper order to match the Japanese.【表現と文法の知識・技能】

(各3点)

1. 次の文章を読んで問いに答えなさい。

(and / passage / read / the following) answer the questions.

_____

2. 入館は閉館時間の30分前まで可能です。

Admission is (allowed / before / until / 30 minutes) closing time.

_____

3. その角を右に曲がると, そのお寺がありますよ。

You (find / if / the temple / will) you turn right at the corner.

_____

E Read the following passage and answer the questions below.

"Super Clone Cultural Properties" Special Exhibition

You will find a lot of important insights (1) you encounter our "cloned" artworks: "Super Clone Cultural Properties."

Dates: November 18 (2) December 28

Opening hours: 10:00–17:30 (Admission ends 30 minutes (3) closing time.)

Closed: Mondays (except national holidays)

Place: The Basement Gallery of Daiichi Bldg.

Admission:	Adult (general)	¥800
	Student*	¥400
	Child (age 12 and under)	Free
	Senior (age 65 and older)*	¥400

*A discount (4)(available / if / is / show / you) a photo ID.

For further information, visit the following site:

www.daiichigallery.org

David: What are you looking at, Kumi?

Kumi: This is about a special art exhibition.

David: Sounds interesting!

Kumi: Do you know anything about "cloned" artworks?

David: Hmm … I don't think I do.

Kumi: Then, (5)(don't / go / to / we / why) the gallery together this weekend?

1. 空所(1)～(3)に入る最も適当な語をそれぞれ選びなさい。【語彙の知識】　　　（各2点）

　ア. before　　　イ. for　　　ウ. to　　　エ. when

　(1) (　　　)　(2) (　　　)　(3) (　　　)

2. 下線部(4)，(5)の(　　)内の語を適切に並べかえなさい。【表現の知識】　　　（各3点）

　(4) _____

　(5) _____

3. 次の問いに英語で答えなさい。【内容についての思考力・判断力・表現力】　　　（各4点）

　(1) If Kumi needs further information, where can she find it?

　_____

　(2) What does David think about the special art exhibition?

　_____

"Cloning" Cultural Properties

Part 2

/50

A Translate the English into Japanese and the Japanese into English.【語彙の知識】(各1点)

1. conflict 名 B1   [   ]   2. _____ 名 B2   天井

3. _____ 動 A2   …を破壊する   4. _____ 名 B1   洞窟

5. preserve 動 B1   [   ]   6. pioneer 名   [   ]

B Choose the word whose underlined part is pronounced differently from the other three.【発音の知識】(各2点)

1. ア. c<u>ei</u>ling   イ. p<u>eo</u>ple   ウ. prof<u>e</u>ssor   エ. s<u>e</u>nior

2. ア. cl<u>o</u>ne   イ. c<u>o</u>nflict   ウ. c<u>o</u>py   エ. pr<u>o</u>perty

3. ア. B<u>u</u>ddha   イ. c<u>ou</u>ntry   ウ. c<u>u</u>ltural   エ. p<u>u</u>blic

C Complete the following English sentences to match the Japanese.【表現の知識】(各3点)

1. 大勢の人がその文化遺産を訪れる。

   A (   ) (   ) (   ) people visit the cultural heritage site.

2. 君はそのままでとてもきれいだよ。

   You look pretty (   ) (   ) (   ).

3. 新しいものもあれば古いものもある。

   (   ) (   ) new, and others are old.

D Arrange the words in the proper order to match the Japanese.【表現と文法の知識・技能】

(各3点)

1. 一人で練習をするのと人前で演じるのは異なる。

   Practicing alone (different / from / is / performing) in front of others.

   _____

2. ケーキはお父さんが切ってくれているよ。

   The cake (being / by / cut / is) your dad.

   _____

3. その山の頂上から見ると，私たちの学校はとても小さく見える。

   (from / of / seen / the mountain / the top), our school looks very small.

   _____

Read the following passage and answer the questions below.

It is very hard to keep cultural properties as (1)they are. Some are damaged during conflicts. Attacked by the Taliban, statues and ceiling paintings of Buddhas at Bamiyan in Afghanistan were destroyed in 2001. (2) are harmed due to tourists. Buddhist caves in Dunhuang, China, are gradually (3)(being / by / damaged / large / the) numbers of tourists.

How can we preserve cultural properties and show them to the public? "Super Clone Cultural Properties" can solve this problem. Professor Masaaki Miyasako is a pioneer in this "cloning" technology. He (4) artworks of all ages and countries.

Some people have negative opinions about "copied" art. However, Miyasako's team respects the DNA of the original artworks. The production process of cloning artworks (5)(copying / different / from / is / quite) things.

1. 下線部(1)が指すものは何ですか。英語で答えなさい。【内容についての思考力・判断力・表現力】(2 点)

2. 空所(2)に入る最も適切な語(句)を選びなさい。【語彙と表現の知識】(2 点)
　　ア. Another　　　　イ. Other　　　　　ウ. Others　　　　エ. The others

3. 下線部(3), (5)の(　　)内の語を適切に並べかえなさい。【表現と文法の知識】(各 3 点)
　　(3)
　　(5)

4. 空所(4)に入る最も適当な語句を選びなさい。【語彙と文法の知識】(2 点)
　　ア. tries to revive　　　　　　　　イ. tries to reviving
　　ウ. trying to revive　　　　　　　エ. trying to reviving

5. 次の問いに英語で答えなさい。【内容についての思考力・判断力・表現力】(各 4 点)
　　(1) Why is it hard to keep cultural properties as they are?

　　(2) What does professor Miyasako try to do?

"Cloning" Cultural Properties   Part 3

/50

A Translate the English into Japanese and the Japanese into English.【語彙の知識】(各1点)

1. _____ 動 B1 …を復元する   2. _____ 動 …を補足する

3. academic 形 B1   [   ]   4. _____ 副 B1 綿密に

5. convey 動 B1   [   ]   6. creator 名 B1   [   ]

B Choose the word which has primary stress on a different syllable from the other three.【アクセントの知識】(各2点)

1. ア. con-vey   イ. re-fer   ウ. re-store   エ. stat-ue

2. ア. com-ple-ment   イ. Jap-a-nese   ウ. pi-o-neer   エ. re-pro-duce

3. ア. ac-a-dem-ic   イ. Af-ghan-i-stan ウ. a-vail-a-ble   エ. o-rig-i-nal

C Complete the following English sentences to match the Japanese.【表現と文法の知識】(各3点)

1. 彼らはうまく解決策を見つけることができた。

   They (   ) (   ) finding a solution.

2. 詳細は添付ファイルをご参照ください。

   (   ) (   ) the attached file for details.

3. 彼はたくさんの困難を乗り越えてきたそうだ。

   It is said that he has (   ) (   ) many difficulties.

D Arrange the words in the proper order to match the Japanese.【表現と文法の知識・技能】(各3点)

1. 彼女はピアノだけでなくギターも演奏する。

   She plays (also / but / not / only / the guitar / the piano).

   _____

2. あれが, 彼女が昨日話していた人だよ。

   That is the person (about / she / talked / who) yesterday.

   _____

3. ここが10年前に私が住んでいた町だ。

   This is (I / in / lived / the town) ten years ago.

   _____

E Read the following passage and answer the questions below.

In 2017, Miyasako's team (1) in cloning the *Shaka Triad* statue of Horyuji Temple. Team members not only reproduced the statue but also restored missing parts.

There were (2)(difficulties / had / Miyasako / to / which) get over. His team was not able to take pictures of the back of the statue. In order to clone the statue, team members complemented information about (3)(by / data / it / saved / using) and academic insights. Miyasako said, "We aim to revive the statue, (4)(refer) to professionals' advice and old books."

When the statue was first created, it was probably shining gold. Miyasako wants to clone the statue (5) closely to the original the next time. He thinks that his cloned artwork should convey the hearts of the creators at that time.

1. 空所(1)に入る最も適当な語(句)を選びなさい。【語彙と表現の知識】 （2点）

　　ア. succeeded 　　　イ. success 　　　　ウ. successful 　　　エ. was succeeded

2. 下線部(2), (3)の(　　)内の語を適切に並べかえなさい。【表現と文法の知識】 （各3点）

　　(2)

　　(3)

3. 下線部(4)の語を適切な形に変えなさい。【表現と文法の知識】 （2点）

4. 空所(5)に入る最も適切な語句を選びなさい。【語彙と文法の知識】 （2点）

　　ア. even more 　　　イ. more even 　　　　ウ. more very 　　　エ. very more

5. 次の問いに英語で答えなさい。【内容についての思考力・判断力・表現力】 （各4点）

　　(1) What did Miyasako's team members do with missing parts of the *Shaka Triad* statue?

　　(2) What does Miyasako want his cloned artwork to convey?

"Cloning" Cultural Properties   Part 4

/50

A Translate the English into Japanese and the Japanese into English. 【語彙の知識】（各1点）

1. ＿＿＿＿＿ 名   芥子   2. detail 名 A2   [   ]

3. statue 名 A2   [   ]   4. ＿＿＿＿＿ 名 A2   展覧会

5. technique 名 B1   [   ]   6. ＿＿＿＿＿ 名   職人技

B Choose the word whose underlined part is pronounced differently from the other three. 【発音の知識】 （各2点）

1. ア. cherry   イ. China   ウ. technique   エ. touch

2. ア. artisanship   イ. basement   ウ. closely   エ. insight

3. ア. collect   イ. detail   ウ. even   エ. team

C Complete the following English sentences to match the Japanese. 【語彙と表現の知識】

（各3点）

1. いつも彼女のことを考えています。

I'm thinking about her (   ) (   ) (   ).

2. 彼らは同時に笑いだした。

They started to laugh (   ) (   ) (   )

(   ).

3. このプロジェクターがあれば，リビングをホームシアターに変えることができます。

(   ) this projector, you can turn your living room into a home

theater.

D Arrange the words in the proper order to match the Japanese. 【表現と文法の知識・技能】

（各3点）

1. 私たちは子供たちのために働くことが好きな人を探しています。

We are looking for (like / those / to / who) work for the benefit of children.

2. 集中して仕事ができる部屋がほしい。

I want (a / I / in / room / which) can concentrate on my work.

3. 一緒に働いている人たちは，私にとても親切です。

(I / the people / whom / with / work) are very kind to me.

E Read the following passage and answer the questions below.

Miyasako also reproduced Tawaraya Sotatsu's *Cherry Blossoms and Poppies*. His team used a camera (1) all the details of the painting could be collected. Thanks to the cloning technology, people can see the cloned work in its original place at all times. (2), the original can be preserved in a different place.

The Fifer, a famous painting by Edouard Manet, was reproduced not only as a painting but also as a statue. At an exhibition, even (3)(could / not / see / those / who) well could touch the statue and appreciate the work.

When Miyasako clones cultural properties, he values traditional techniques of artisanship. He also uses the (4) technologies. With the cloning technology, we may be able to preserve cultural properties and (5)(available / make / the public / them / to) forever.

1. 空所(1), (2)に入る最も適当な語(句)を選びなさい。【表現と文法の知識】　　　（各2点）

  (1) ア. that　　　　イ. which　　　　ウ. with when　　　　エ. with which

  (2) ア. At first　　　イ. At last　　　ウ. At the same time　　　エ. However

2. 下線部(3), (5)の(　　)内の語句を適切に並べかえなさい。【表現と文法の知識】　　（各3点）

  (3) _____

  (5) _____

3. 空所(4)に入る最も適当な語を選びなさい。【語彙と表現の知識】　　　　　　　（2点）

  ア. last　　　　　　イ. late　　　　　　ウ. latest　　　　　エ. latter

4. 次の問いに英語で答えなさい。【内容についての思考力・判断力・表現力】　　　（各4点）

  (1) What was a good point of reproducing *the Fifer* as a statue?

  _____

  (2) What may be possible with cloning technology?

  _____

A Translate the English into Japanese and the Japanese into English. 【語彙の知識】 (各1点)

1. _____ 形 B1 原子力の   2. _____ 形 B2 倫理に反する

3. _____ 名 慰霊碑   4. candle 名 B1 [   ]

5. clash 名 [   ]   6. suffering 名 B2 [   ]

B Choose the word which has primary stress on a different syllable from the other three. 【アクセントの知識】 (各2点)

1. ア. cer-e-mo-ny   イ. dis-cov-er-y   ウ. en-vi-ron-ment   エ. me-mo-ri-al

2. ア. con-sid-er   イ. con-ven-ience   ウ. de-ci-sion   エ. Vat-i-can

3. ア. cen-o-taph   イ. im-mor-al   ウ. o-pen-ing   エ. the-a-ter

C Complete the following English sentences to match the Japanese. 【表現と文法の知識】 (各3点)

1. 約5万人がそのコンサートに参加した。

   About 50,000 people (   ) the (   ).

2. 武志は真司に箱を運ぶよう頼んだ。

   Takeshi (   ) Shinji (   ) carry the box.

3. あなたの人生が幸せでいっぱいでありますように。

   (   ) your (   ) be full of happiness.

D Arrange the words in the proper order to match the Japanese. 【表現と文法の知識・技能】 (各3点)

1. この試験では辞書の使用は認められていない。

   (dictionaries / is / not / of / permitted / the use) in this examination.

   _____

2. テーブルの上にリンゴとブドウがあった。

   On (and / apples / grapes / the table / were).

   _____

3. 紘一はいつも彼女を幸せにする。

   (always / happy / her / Koichi / makes).

   _____

E Read the following passage and answer the questions below.

"The use of atomic energy for purposes of war is a crime. It is immoral." Pope Francis said this at Hiroshima Peace Memorial Park on November 24, 2019. (1) that day, the Meeting for Peace was held in front of the Cenotaph for the A-bomb Victims.

About 2,000 people attended the meeting. Among them was a Japanese High School Student Peace Ambassador. (2)(a light / handed / she / the Pope), and he lit a candle. She had met him before in the Vatican and had asked him to come to Hiroshima. She said, "I'm (3)(happy / his visit / if / made / our wish / possible)."

At the meeting, the Pope gave his message to the world. "Never again war, never again the clash of arms, never again so much suffering! (4) peace come in our time and to our world."

1. 空所(1)に入る最も適当な語を選びなさい。【表現の知識】　　　　　　　　　（3点）
　　ア. At　　　　　　イ. In　　　　　　ウ. On　　　　　　エ. With

2. 下線部(2)の(　　)内の語句を適切に並べかえなさい。【表現と文法の知識】　　（3点）

　　_____

3. 下線部(3)の(　　)内の語句を適切に並べかえなさい。【表現と文法の知識】　　（3点）

　　_____

4. 空所(4)に入る最も適当な語を選びなさい。【語彙と表現の知識】　　　　　　　（3点）
　　ア. Can　　　　　　イ. May　　　　　　ウ. Shall　　　　　　エ. Will

5. 次の問いに英語で答えなさい。【内容についての思考力・判断力・表現力】　　（各4点）
　　(1) What did Pope Francis say at Hiroshima Peace Memorial Park on November 24, 2019?

　　_____

　　(2) Did a Japanese High School Student Peace Ambassador meet Pope Francis before November 24, 2019?

　　_____

A Translate the English into Japanese and the Japanese into English.【語彙の知識】(各1点)

1. _____ 名 B2　爆撃
2. _____ 名 B1　甥
3. _____ 名　武装解除
4. campaign 名 B2　[　　　　　　　]
5. throughout 前 B1　[　　　　　　　]
6. eliminate 動 B1　[　　　　　　　]

B Choose the word which has primary stress on a different syllable from the other three.【アクセントの知識】 (各2点)

1. ア. bomb-ing　　イ. cam-paign　　ウ. pump-kin　　エ. sun-shine
2. ア. cof-fee　　イ. con-nect　　ウ. na-ture　　エ. neph-ew
3. ア. lec-ture　　イ. pro-duce (動詞)　ウ. re-peat　　エ. through-out

C Complete the following English sentences to match the Japanese.【表現の知識】 (各3点)

1. 芳恵は昨日の練習に参加した。

Yoshie (　　　　　　) part (　　　　　　) yesterday's practice.

2. 恵美は文化祭で重要な役割を担っている。

Megumi (　　　　　) an important (　　　　　) in the cultural festival.

3. 彼女の平和の訴えは全員に感動を与えた。

Her (　　　　) (　　　　　　) peace impressed everyone.

D Arrange the words in the proper order to match the Japanese.【表現と文法の知識・技能】

(各3点)

1. 昨日の事故で多くの人が亡くなりました。

(in / many people / lost / the / their lives / yesterday's accident).

_____

2. あなたがこのようなつらいときを経験しないことを願います。

I hope (a / difficult / experience / such / will not / you) time.

_____

3. 田中先生の言葉はこのクラスの生徒に影響を与えました。

(in / influenced / Mr. Tanaka's / the students / this class / words).

_____

E Read the following passage and answer the questions below.

Setsuko Thurlow also took part in the Meeting for Peace. When she was 13, she experienced the atomic bombing in Hiroshima. Her sister and nephew, as (1) as many of her classmates, lost their lives at that time.

Thurlow believed that her experience as an A-bomb survivor would (2) an important role. She started a nuclear disarmament campaign in the 1950s. (3)(a lot / gave / lectures / of / she / the world / throughout). Her activities even influenced world leaders.

Thurlow listened to Pope Francis speak at the meeting. She hoped that his appeal for world peace would help people (4) it even more. She said, "I'm sure his message will spread all over the world. Every citizen must take his message as a starting point and take action to eliminate nuclear weapons."

1. 空所(1), (2)に入る最も適当な語を選びなさい。【表現の知識】　　　　　（各3点）

　　(1) ア. good　　　イ. many　　　ウ. much　　　エ. well
　　(2) ア. have　　　イ. help　　　ウ. play　　　エ. work

2. 下線部(3)の(　　)内の語句を適切に並べかえなさい。【表現と文法の知識】　（3点）

　　--

3. 空所(4)に入る最も適当な語(句)を選びなさい。【文法の知識】　　　　　（3点）

　　ア. seek　　　イ. seeking　　　ウ. sought　　　エ. to sought

4. 次の問いに英語で答えなさい。【内容についての思考力・判断力・表現力】　（各4点）

　　(1) What did Thurlow join in Hiroshima?

　　--

　　(2) What did Thurlow start in the 1950s?

　　--

Peace Messages from Hiroshima Part 3

/50

A Translate the English into Japanese and the Japanese into English. 【語彙の知識】 (各1点)

1. ＿＿＿＿＿＿ 名 B2　証言

2. ＿＿＿＿＿＿ 動 B1　…を強調する

3. ＿＿＿＿＿＿ 動 B1　…だと主張する

4. dawn 名 B2　[　　　　　　]

5. warfare 名　[　　　　　　]

6. awakening 名　[　　　　　　]

B Choose the word which has primary stress on a different syllable from the other three. 【アクセントの知識】 (各2点)

1. ア. be-gin-ning　　イ. em-pha-size　　ウ. lau-re-ate　　エ. pres-i-dent

2. ア. ad-ven-ture　　イ. ar-ti-cle　　ウ. a-tom-ic　　エ. con-sid-er

3. ア. fu-ture　　イ. heav-y　　ウ. in-sist　　エ. war-fare

C Complete the following English sentences to match the Japanese. 【表現と文法の知識】

(各3点)

1. 彼らはその事故の証言をします。

They will (　　　　　) (　　　　　) to the accident.

2. 年を取るにつれて，責任も大きくなります。

As we (　　　　) (　　　　　), we have more responsibility.

3. 西村さんは山口の有名な俳優として知られている。

Mr. Nishimura is (　　　　) (　　　　　) a famous actor in Yamaguchi.

D Arrange the words in the proper order to match the Japanese. 【表現と文法の知識・技能】

(各3点)

1. 康介はもうこのグループと一緒に歌うことはない。

Kosuke (longer / no / sings / songs / this group / with).

2. 彼はこのバス停の名前を変えるべきだと主張した。

He (change / insisted / should / that / the name / they) of this bus stop.

3. 大統領は他国の首相にお互いに助け合うことを求めた。

The President (called / countries / of / on / the other / the prime ministers / to) help each other.

E Read the following passage and answer the questions below.

In 2016, Barack Obama, the U.S. president and the 2009 Nobel Laureate in Peace, came to Hiroshima. (1)(he / president / sitting / the first / to / visit / was) the atomic-bombed city. He knew atomic bomb survivors were getting older and said in his speech, "Someday the voices of the *hibakusha* will no longer be with us to bear witness."

Obama emphasized the (2) of science. He insisted that science should be focused on improving life, not eliminating it. This is part of the lesson of Hiroshima. We shouldn't keep our eyes turned (3) from the lesson anymore.

In his speech, Obama called on world leaders to choose a world with no more war. (4)"Hiroshima and Nagasaki are known (A) as the dawn of atomic warfare, (B) as the start of our own moral awakening." This is the future, Obama said, "we can choose."

1. 下線部(1)の(　　)内の語句を適切に並べかえなさい。【表現の知識】　　　　　　　　（3点）

_____

2. 空所(2)に入る最も適当な語を選びなさい。【語彙の知識】　　　　　　　　（2点）
　　ア. importance　　イ. important　　ウ. imported　　エ. importing

3. 空所(3)に入る最も適当な語を答えなさい。【語彙と表現の知識】　　　　　　　　（3点）
　　(　　　　　　　)

4. 下線部(4)の空所(A), (B)に入る最も適当な語をそれぞれ選びなさい。【表現と文法の知識】（各2点）
　　ア. and　　　　イ. but　　　　ウ. not　　　　エ. or
　　(A) (　　　)　　(B) (　　　)

5. 次の問いに英語で答えなさい。【内容についての思考力・判断力・表現力】　　　　　　（各4点）
　　(1) Before Barack Obama, how many U.S. presidents visited Hiroshima?

_____

　　(2) Is it possible for us to listen to the witness of the *hibakusha* forever?

_____

A Translate the English into Japanese and the Japanese into English. 【語彙の知識】(各1点)

1. _____ 副 B1 すぐに

2. significant 形 A2 [   ]

3. _____ 動 B2 …を撤廃する

4. terrifying 形 B2 [   ]

5. _____ 形 B1 印象的な

6. scientific 形 A2 [   ]

B Choose the word which has primary stress on a different syllable from the other three. 【アクセントの知識】(各2点)

1. ア. a-wak-en-ing　　イ. de-vel-op-ment　　ウ. sig-nif-i-cant　　エ. ter-ri-fy-ing

2. ア. a-bol-ish　　イ. di-a-ry　　ウ. in-ter-est　　エ. pos-si-ble

3. ア. im-pres-sive　　イ. pol-lu-tion　　ウ. po-si-tion　　エ. re-al-ize

C Complete the following English sentences to match the Japanese. 【表現の知識】(各3点)

1. もしよければ，この文を取り除きたいのですが。

I would like to (　　　　　　) (　　　　　　) of this sentence if you don't mind.

2. うわさをすれば影（←鬼の話をすればきっと鬼が現れる）。

(　　　　　　) (　　　　　　) the Devil and he is sure to appear.

3. この問題に取り組んでもらえませんか。

Could you (　　　　　　) (　　　　　　) this problem?

D Arrange the words in the proper order to match the Japanese. 【表現と文法の知識・技能】

(各3点)

1. 私はあなたとこの情報を共有できるよ。

(can / I / share / the information / with / you).

_____

2. 苦情はすべて支配人が処理するでしょう。

(all / be / complaints / dealt / will / with) by the manager.

_____

3. 私たちはこの行事には問題がたくさんあるという事実に気づくべきだ。

(realize / should / that / the fact / this event / we) has many problems.

_____

E Read the following passage and answer the questions below.

David: The media reported a lot on the Pope's message in Hiroshima. The question is, will the message help to get rid of nuclear weapons?

Kumi: Not immediately. But the Pope's visit is a significant step.

Manabu: Yes, (1)(abolish / his call / nuclear / spread / to / weapons) all over the world.

Vivian: He said, "(2)How can we speak of peace even as we build terrifying new weapons?" Very (3).

David: Do you think world leaders will listen and share the ideal of peace with him?

Kumi: I'm not sure. But we should realize the fact that (4)(be / leaders / like / people / us / will / younger) someday. The world will gradually change.

David: How true! So, what can you do now?

Vivian: We have to learn more about peace and war. We should also learn to have high morals to deal with scientific developments.

1. 下線部(1)の(　　)内の語句を適切に並べかえなさい。【表現と文法の知識】　　　　（3点）

　　　　...

2. 下線部(2)を日本語にしなさい。【表現と文法の知識】　　　　（3点）

　　　　...

3. 空所(3)に入る最も適当な語を選びなさい。【語彙の知識】　　　　（3点）

　　ア. helpful　　　　　イ. impressive　　　　ウ. influence　　　　エ. interested

4. 下線部(4)の(　　)内の語を適切に並べかえなさい。【表現と文法の知識】　　　　（3点）

　　　　...

5. 次の問いに英語で答えなさい。【内容についての思考力・判断力・表現力】　　　　（各4点）

　　(1) Does Kumi think the Pope's message will help to get rid of nuclear weapons immediately?

　　　　...

　　(2) Who thinks we must learn more about peace and war?

　　　　...

Invigorating Our Local Community

Part 1

/50

A Translate the English into Japanese and the Japanese into English. 【語彙の知識】 (各1点)

1. _____ 動　　…を活気づける
2. gourmet 形　　[　　　　　　　　　　]
3. _____ 名 B1　材料，食材
4. contestant 名　　[　　　　　　　　　　]
5. panel 名 B2　　[　　　　　　　　　　]
6. _____ 副 B1　その結果

B Choose the word which has primary stress on a different syllable from the other three. 【アクセントの知識】

(各2点)

1. ア. chal-lenge　　イ. gour-met　　ウ. se-lect　　エ. towns-people
2. ア. con-test-ant　　イ. fish-er-man　　ウ. flex-i-bly　　エ. rec-i-pe
3. ア. com-mu-ni-ty　　イ. con-se-quent-ly　　ウ. in-gre-di-ent　　エ. in-vig-or-ate

C Complete the following English sentences to match the Japanese. 【表現の知識】 (各3点)

1. 審査員団は彼を勝者に選んだ。

The (　　　　　　　　) (　　　　　　　　　　) judges selected him as the winner.

2. 彼らは私たち全員にすばらしい料理を出してくれた。

They (　　　　　　　　) a wonderful meal (　　　　　　　　) us all.

3. 結果的に，私たちはその後の人生を共に過ごした。

(　　　　　　　　), we spent the rest of our lives together.

D Arrange the words in the proper order to match the Japanese. 【表現と文法の知識・技能】

(各3点)

1. 自転車に乗りながらスマートフォンを使ってはいけない。

You must not (cycling / smartphone / use / your / while).

_____

2. サラダと一緒に食べると，このチキンはとても美味しいよ。

(eaten / salad / when / with), this chicken is very good.

_____

3. 失敗からたくさんのことを学ぶものだよ。あきらめないで。

We (a lot / from / learn / making / mistakes). Don't give up.

_____

E Read the following passage and answer the questions below.

A cooking competition among high school students in Hokkaido invigorates the local community. The competition is called "The Challenge Gourmet Contest." In this contest, high school students compete in making their own original recipes and using their cooking skills (1) local ingredients.

Students flexibly develop their ideas to create recipes for the contest. On the day of the contest, contestants serve their original food to local people. A panel of judges tries all the food, selects their favorites, and (2)(record) their votes. (3), this type of contest brings energy to the local community through food.

A man in a local fishermen's organization says, "(4)(events / is / of / one / the biggest / the contest) in this town." The high school students entertain the townspeople. At the same time, the students learn a lot more from (5)(participate) in a community event.

1. 空所(1)に入る最も適当な語句を選びなさい。【語彙と文法の知識】　　　　　（3点）

ア. while they used　　イ. while they using　　ウ. while used　　エ. while using

2. 下線部(2), (5)の語を適切な形に変えなさい。【表現と文法の知識】　　　　　（各2点）

(2) ....

(5) ....

3. 空所(3)に入る最も適当な語を選びなさい。【語彙の知識】　　　　　（2点）

ア. Consequently　　イ. However　　　　ウ. Instead　　エ. Unfortunately

4. 下線部(4)の(　　)内の語句を適切に並べかえなさい。【表現の知識】　　　　　（3点）

....

5. 次の問いに英語で答えなさい。【内容についての思考力・判断力・表現力】　　　　　（各4点）

(1) Who competes in "The Challenge Gourmet Contest"?

....

(2) What does the contest bring to the local people?

....

Invigorating Our Local Community **Part 2**

/50

A Translate the English into Japanese and the Japanese into English.【語彙の知識】(各1点)

1. ＿＿＿＿＿＿＿ 图 A2　機会，チャンス
2. contribution 图 B1　[　　　　　]
3. ＿＿＿＿＿＿＿ 图 B1　衰え，衰退
4. indispensable 形 B2　[　　　　　]
5. maintain 動 B1　[　　　　　]
6. ＿＿＿＿＿＿＿ 图　活力，活気

B Choose the word which has primary stress on a different syllable from the other three.【アクセントの知識】(各2点)

1. ア. ag-ing　　　イ. de-cline　　　ウ. main-tain　　　エ. re-sult
2. ア. fa-vor-ite　　イ. in-dus-try　　ウ. or-gan-ize　　エ. out-stand-ing
3. ア. char-ac-ter-is-tic　　　　　イ. in-dis-pen-sa-ble
　 ウ. in-di-vid-u-al　　　　　　エ. op-por-tu-ni-ty

C Complete the following English sentences to match the Japanese.【表現の知識】(各3点)

1. 規則にこだわる人もいれば，そうでない人もいる。

    Some people (　　　　　) (　　　　　) rules, and others don't.

2. 今週末は家にいて子供たちの世話をする予定です。

    I am going to stay home and (　　　　　) (　　　　　) my children this weekend.

3. これらの本は私の研究に欠かせません。

    These books (　　　　) (　　　　) (　　　　) my research.

D Arrange the words in the proper order to match the Japanese.【表現と文法の知識・技能】

(各3点)

1. そのとき，私は知らずに彼女を傷つけてしまった。

    At that time, I (her / hurt / realizing / without) it.

2. この食べ物は日本では健康によいと思われている。

    This food (be / believed / healthy / is / to) in Japan.

3. 彼は彼女のことを誤解していたようだ。

    He (have / her / misunderstood / seems / to).

E Read the following passage and answer the questions below.

High school students in the contest get valuable training to enter the adult world. In (1)(manage) to organize an event with local adults, they can get an opportunity to change from "being served and cared for" (2) "serving and caring for" someone. As a result, they realize that society needs (3)them.

Local people hope that high school students will make contributions to their communities. Today's aging society often (4)(declines / in / leads / local / to) industries. Many people think that the power of youths is indispensable for solving local problems and for maintaining the special values of their communities.

Young people have their own outstanding ideas and the vitality to create new things. They can show their new ways of thinking without sticking to old customs. In the "gourmet contest," such characteristics of the high school students (5)(created / have / interesting / seem / to) and delicious food.

1. 下線部(1)の語を適切な形に変えなさい。【表現と文法の知識】　　　　　　　（2点）

　　　　　

2. 空所(2)に入る最も適当な語を選びなさい。【語彙の知識】　　　　　　　　　　（2点）
　　ア. and　　　　　　　イ. for　　　　　　　ウ. in　　　　　　　エ. to

3. 下線部(3)は何を指していますか。英語で答えなさい。【内容についての思考力・判断力・表現力】（2点）

　　　　　

4. 下線部(4), (5)の（　　）内の語を適切に並べかえなさい。【表現と文法の知識】　（各3点）
　　(4)　　　　　
　　(5)　　　　　

5. 次の問いに英語で答えなさい。【内容についての思考力・判断力・表現力】　　（各4点）
　　(1) Who hopes for young people's contributions to their communities?

　　　　　

　　(2) Do young people stick to old customs?

A Translate the English into Japanese and the Japanese into English. 【語彙の知識】 (各1点)

1. meanwhile 副 B1 [   ] 2. _____ 名 持続可能性

3. _____ 動 B2 努力する 4. _____ 名 B2 参加，加入

5. stimulate 動 B2 [   ] 6. declare 動 B1 [   ]

B Choose the word which has primary stress on a different syllable from the other three. 【アクセントの知識】 (各2点)

1. ア. ac-cept　　　イ. coun-try　　　ウ. de-clare　　　エ. e-vent

2. ア. an-y-thing　　イ. con-trib-ute　　ウ. pres-i-dent　　エ. stim-u-late

3. ア. grad-u-a-tion　イ. in-au-gu-ral　　ウ. sus-tain-a-ble　エ. vi-tal-i-ty

C Complete the following English sentences to match the Japanese. 【表現の知識】 (各3点)

1. 一生懸命勉強しなさい。一方で，しっかり睡眠をとることも大切です。

You should study hard. (   ), it is also important to have a good sleep.

2. そんな人とまだ連絡を取っているのですか。

Do you still (   ) (   ) (   ) with such a person?

3. 彼は家族のためにもっとお金を稼ぐよう努力した。

He (   ) (   ) earn more money for his family.

D Arrange the words in the proper order to match the Japanese. 【表現と文法の知識・技能】

(各3点)

1. 何か問題があれば，私に電話をしさえすれば大丈夫だよ。

If you are in trouble, all (do / have / to / you) is call me.

2. そのジャケット自体はそんなに悪くはないよ。

(is / itself / not / the jacket) that bad.

3. 過去のことにこだわり続けるべきではない。

You should not (about / keep / the past / thinking).

E Read the following passage and answer the questions below.

Today, there are many local communities (1) the number of young people has been decreasing. Meanwhile, in one survey, about 70% of high school students answered that they wanted to stay in (2)(in / keep / or / touch / with) their hometowns after graduation. Young people value local communities and can be helpful for (3)their sustainability.

Even while in high school, students can start contributing in the following ways. First, they can use what they learn at school and strive to do (4) they can do to help. Second, their participation itself can stimulate local people.

Once John F. Kennedy, the 35th U.S. president, declared in his inaugural address, "Ask not what your country can do for you. Ask what you can do for your country." Now, (5)(all / do / have / is / to / we) keep learning and thinking about this: What can we do for our local communities?

1. 空所(1)に入る最も適当な語を選びなさい。【文法の知識】　　　　　　　　　　（2点）

　ア. what　　　　　イ. where　　　　　ウ. which　　　　エ. whose

2. 下線部(2), (5)の(　　)内の語を適切に並べかえなさい。【表現と文法の知識】　　　（各3点）

　(2) _____

　(5) _____

3. 下線部(3)が指すものとして最も適当なものを選びなさい。

　　　　　　　　　　　　　　　　　　　　　　　【内容についての思考力・判断力・表現力】（2点）

　ア. high school students'　　　　　　イ. local communities'
　ウ. local people's　　　　　　　　　　エ. young people's

4. 空所(4)に入る最も適当な語を選びなさい。【文法の知識】　　　　　　　　　　（2点）

　ア. what　　　　　イ. when　　　　　ウ. where　　　　エ. whose

5. 次の問いに英語で答えなさい。【内容についての思考力・判断力・表現力】　　　（各4点）

　(1) What can high school students use to contribute to local communities?

　_____

　(2) What should we keep thinking about?

　_____

Invigorating Our Local Community Part 4

/50

A Translate the English into Japanese and the Japanese into English.【語彙の知識】（各1点）

1. regularly 副 A2　　[　　　　　] 　2. ＿＿＿＿＿＿ 形 B1　生の，ライブの

3. mall 名 A2　　　[　　　　　] 　4. ＿＿＿＿＿＿ 名 A2　観客，聴衆

5. ＿＿＿＿＿ 副 A2　たいてい，ほとんど　6. limited 形 B1　　[　　　　　]

B Choose the word whose underlined part is pronounced differently from the other three.【発音の知識】　　　　　　　　　　　　　　　　　　（各2点）

1. ア. Brisbane　　　イ. limited　　　ウ. live（形容詞）　　エ. stimulate

2. ア. boat　　　　イ. broadcasting　　ウ. local　　　　エ. mostly

3. ア. audience　　　イ. inaugural　　　ウ. mall　　　　エ. valuable

C Complete the following English sentences to match the Japanese.【表現と文法の知識】

（各3点）

1. もっと時間があれば，もっと野球を練習できるのに。

  If we had more time, we (　　　　　) (　　　　　) baseball.

2. この風習はこの地域に限られたものです。

  This custom (　　　　　) (　　　　　) (　　　　　) this area.

3. スタジアムには大勢の観客がいた。

  There was a (　　　　　) (　　　　　) in the stadium.

D Arrange the words in the proper order to match the Japanese.【表現と文法の知識・技能】

（各3点）

1. 過去に戻ることは不可能だ。

  It is (back / go / impossible / to) to the past.

2. 電車に乗っていたら，もっと早く家に着いただろうに。

  If I had caught the train, I (could / gotten / have / home) earlier.

3. 暇があったら，彼女をデートに誘ったのに。

  If (been / free / had / I), I would have asked her out.

E Read the following passage and answer the questions below.

Interviewer: Our school's light music club regularly hosts live concerts at a local shopping mall. Everyone around here looks forward to it, and many people come each time. Let's listen to what the club members have to say now. ... Well, why did you start (1)such an activity?

Kumi: (2)(a lot of people / listen / to / wanted / we) to our music because the audience in school events is mostly limited to friends and family.

Interviewer: Have you found anything through this activity?

Taro: Yes! At the first concert, (3)(find / surprised / to / we / were) so many people were interested in high school students' activities. We couldn't have noticed (4)this if we had played only at school.

Interviewer: What do you want to do in the future?

Vivian: When I go back to my home country, I'd like to play music together with the local people.

Interviewer: Thank you so much for your time.

1. 下線部(1)は何を指していますか。日本語で説明しなさい。【内容についての思考力・判断力・表現力】

（3点）

_____

2. 下線部(2), (3)の(　　)内の語句を適切に並べかえなさい。【表現の知識】　　（各3点）

(2) _____

(3) _____

3. 下線部(4)は何を指していますか。日本語で説明しなさい。【内容についての思考力・判断力・表現力】

（3点）

_____

4. 次の問いに英語で答えなさい。【内容についての思考力・判断力・表現力】　　（各4点）

(1) What does the light music club regularly host?

_____

(2) What have the members of the light music club noticed through their activities?

_____

A Translate the English into Japanese and the Japanese into English.【語彙の知識】(各1点)

1. habitat 名 B1　　[　　　　　]　　2. _____ 動 B1　…を助長する

3. _____ 形 A2　害を与える　　4. _____ 名 A2　行動, 行い

5. selfie 名　　[　　　　　]　　6. click 動 A2　　[　　　　　]

B Choose the word which has primary stress on a different syllable from the other three.【アクセントの知識】(各2点)

1. ア. bet-ter　　イ. en-joy　　ウ. harm-ful　　エ. o-ver

2. ア. en-vi-ron-ment　イ. ex-pe-ri-ence　ウ. in-ter-ac-tion　エ. tech-nol-o-gy

3. ア. ar-ti-cle　　イ. be-hav-ior　　ウ. hab-i-tat　　エ. o-pen-ing

C Complete the following English sentences to match the Japanese.【表現と文法の知識】(各3点)

1. この列車は禁煙です。

Smoking (　　　　　　) not (　　　　　　) on this train.

2. トムが私と話していたとき, あなたは何をしていたの？

What (　　　　　) you doing when Tom was (　　　　　) with me?

3. 卓也が今日, なぜお金をたくさん持っているかは遼平が知っていると思うよ。

I think Ryohei (　　　　　) (　　　　　) Takuya has a lot of money today.

D Arrange the words in the proper order to match the Japanese.【表現と文法の知識・技能】(各3点)

1. 孝雄は水泳が好きなようです。

(it / likes / seems / swimming / Takao / that).

_____

2. あなたにここで会うなんて思ってもみなかったです。

Never (did / expect / I / meet / to / you) here.

_____

3. 歯医者に行ったほうがいいですよ。

(a dentist / better / go / had / to / you).

_____

E Read the following passage and answer the questions below.

Doing something that harms animals or their habitats is NOT allowed on our site. You are searching for posts that may promote harmful behavior toward animals or the environment.

Kumi: Hey, I need your help!

David: Hi, Kumi. What's wrong?

Kumi: I (1)(animals / of / photos / see / some / to / wanted) on social media. Then, this pop-up message appeared. What's this?

David: Let me see. "… may promote harmful behavior toward animals or the environment"?! Well, what were you doing (2) it appeared?

Kumi: Nothing special.

David: But … it seems that you did something that might hurt animals.

Kumi: Never (3)(doing / I / of / something / think / would) like that. I just don't understand why I got this message.

David: Hmm … What search words did you use?

Kumi: "Koalaselfie."

David: Um … Sorry, I have no idea. You'd better click on the "Learn More" link for more information.

1. 下線部(1)の( )内の語を適切に並べかえなさい。【表現と文法の知識】 （4点）

2. 空所(2)に入る最も適当な語を選びなさい。【語彙の知識】 （4点）

　　ア. because　　　　イ. if　　　　　　ウ. since　　　　　エ. when

3. 下線部(3)の( )内の語を適切に並べかえなさい。【文法と表現の知識】 （4点）

4. 次の問いに英語で答えなさい。【内容についての思考力・判断力・表現力】 （各4点）

　(1) What is not allowed on the site Kumi visited?

　(2) Did Kumi and David find out the reason for the pop-up message?

The Underside of Wildlife Tourism Part 2

/50

A Translate the English into Japanese and the Japanese into English.【語彙の知識】（各1点）

1. .... 動 B1　ふれあう　　　　2. .... 名 B1　野生生物

3. .... 名 B1　観光業　　　　　4. prevail 動 B2　　　[　　　　　　]

5. underside 名　　　[　　　　　　]　　6. agony 名 B2　　　[　　　　　　]

B Choose the word which has primary stress on a different syllable from the other three.【アクセントの知識】

（各2点）

1. ア. cam-er-a　　　イ. pop-u-lar　　　ウ. ra-di-o　　　エ. va-ca-tion

2. ア. ag-o-ny　　　イ. choc-o-late　　　ウ. in-ter-act　　　エ. me-di-a

3. ア. pre-vail　　　イ. tour-ism　　　ウ. under-side　　　エ. wild-life

C Complete the following English sentences to match the Japanese.【表現と文法の知識】

（各3点）

1. 映画を見て楽しんだかい？

Did you enjoy (　　　　　　) the (　　　　　　)?

2. 都会に住みたい人がいる一方，田舎に住みたい人もいる。

(　　　　　) people want to live in cities, (　　　　　) (　　　　　)
want to live in rural areas.

3. ご存じかもしれませんが，トムは泳ぐのが苦手です。

(　　　　　) you (　　　　　) know, Tom is not good at swimming.

D Arrange the words in the proper order to match the Japanese.【表現と文法の知識・技能】

（各3点）

1. 皆さんと交流できてうれしいです。

I'm (could / happy / I / interact / that / with / you) all.

----

2. 有名な作家と話をしたので，たくさんの本を読みたい気分になりました。

Since I talked with (a famous novelist, / I / inspired / read / to / was) a lot of
books.

----

3. 仕事の手を止めて，リフレッシュする時間をとってください。

Please stop (a moment / and / refresh / take / to / working) yourself.

E Read the following passage and answer the questions below.

What do people like to do when they are (1) vacation? These days, many people enjoy interacting with animals by participating in wildlife tourism. Some people can hold a koala or a sloth in their arms, (2) others can swim with dolphins. During these experiences, they often take selfies with the animals and post the photos online.

This kind of tourism has become extremely popular as social media have prevailed on the Internet. As you may guess, posting selfies with the animals on social media encourages wildlife tourism. Site visitors may be inspired to do the same.

Now, take a moment (3)(think) about the friendly animals that meet with the tourists. Actually, (4)(hidden / is / on / something / the underside / there) of wildlife tourism. Having suffered great agonies caused by human beings, some animals are in terrible health.

1. 空所(1), (2)に入る最も適当な語を選びなさい。【語彙と表現の知識】　　　(各3点)

　(1) ア. at　　　　　イ. in　　　　　ウ. on　　　　　エ. with
　(2) ア. after　　　　イ. before　　　ウ. when　　　　エ. while

2. 下線部(3)の語を適切な形に変えなさい。【表現と文法の知識】　　　(3点)

　　　　　　　　　　　　　　　　　　　　　　　　　　　　

3. 下線部(4)の(　　)内の語句を適切に並べかえなさい。【表現と文法の知識】　(3点)

4. 次の問いに英語で答えなさい。【内容についての思考力・判断力・表現力】　(各4点)

　(1) How do many people enjoy interacting with animals these days?

　(2) What may site visitors be inspired to do?

A Translate the English into Japanese and the Japanese into English.【語彙の知識】(各1点)

1. _____ 名　　(ライオンなどの)子　　2. _____ 動　　寄り添う

3. _____ 動　　爪を抜く　　4. drug 名 A2　　[　　　　　　]

5. illegally 副 B1　　[　　　　　]　　6. jungle 名 B1　　[　　　　　　]

B Choose the word which has primary stress on a different syllable from the other three.【アクセントの知識】(各2点)

1. ア. na-ture　　　イ. re-peat　　　ウ. spe-cial　　　エ. sto-ry

2. ア. at-ten-tion　　イ. cu-ri-ous　　ウ. o-pen-ing　　エ. pop-u-lar

3. ア. be-cause　　　イ. hu-man　　　ウ. meth-od　　　エ. o-ver

C Complete the following English sentences to match the Japanese.【表現と文法の知識】

(各3点)

1. あなたとの出会いで私の人生は変わりました。

The (　　　　　) (　　　　　　　) you changed my life.

2. この動物に寄り添うことができます。

You can (　　　　　) (　　　　　　　) with this animal.

3. 一度中国語の勉強をはじめたら，好きになるでしょう。

(　　　　　) (　　　　　　　) start studying Chinese, you'll love it.

D Arrange the words in the proper order to match the Japanese.【表現と文法の知識・技能】

(各3点)

1. できるだけ早くこの宿題を提出してください。

Please (as / as / hand in / possible / soon / this homework).

_____

2. 彼らのほとんどはその事実を知りません。

(don't / know / most / of / the fact / them).

_____

3. 謙はまるで有名な司会者であるかのように話します。

Ken (a / as / famous / he / if / presenter / talks / were).

_____

E Read the following passage and answer the questions below.

In wildlife tourism, tourists can enjoy encounters with attractive animals. (1), there are adult tigers that are gentle enough for people to touch, and there are tiger cubs that tourists can snuggle up with. In fact, the adult tigers may be declawed, given some special drug, or both. (2)The cubs are taken from their mothers just days after birth so that the mothers can have new babies as soon as possible.

Sloths are popular animals for selfies. They naturally live in tropical forests. However, some sloths are taken illegally from jungles for business purposes. Once they are caught and kept in a cage, (3)(die / often / they / weeks / within).

Most of the tourists don't know these facts. Probably, the animals' behavior appears to them as if the animals (4) also having fun with them. Sadly, this human view may help promote the business.

1. 空所(1)に入る最も適当な語(句)を選びなさい。【語彙と表現の知識】　　　　　　（3点）

　　ア. As a result　　　イ. Besides　　　　ウ. For example　　エ. Thus

2. 下線部(2)を日本語にしなさい。【表現と文法の知識】　　　　　　　　　　　　　（3点）

　　　..

　　　..

3. 下線部(3)の(　　)内の語を適切に並べかえなさい。【表現の知識】　　　　　　（3点）

　　　..

4. 空所(4)に入る最も適当な語(句)を選びなさい。【表現と文法の知識】　　　　　（3点）

　　ア. be　　　　　　　イ. have been　　　ウ. is　　　　　　エ. were

5. 次の問いに英語で答えなさい。【内容についての思考力・判断力・表現力】　　　（各4点）

　　(1) What can tourists do in wildlife tourism?

　　　..

　　(2) Do many people know the facts about wildlife tourism?

　　　..

The Underside of Wildlife Tourism Part 4

/50

A Translate the English into Japanese and the Japanese into English.【語彙の知識】(各1点)

1. _____ 名 B1　責任　　　　　2. _____ 名 B1　生態系

3. moreover 副 B1　　　[　　　　　]　　4. prevailing 形　　　[　　　　　　]

5. single 形 A2　　　　[　　　　　]　　6. _____ 名 B2　虐待

B Choose the word which has primary stress on a different syllable from the other three.【アクセントの知識】(各2点)

1. ア. ben-e-fit　　　イ. med-i-cine　　　ウ. more-o-ver　　　エ. rec-og-nize

2. ア. cam-er-a　　　イ. pas-sen-ger　　　ウ. re-cent-ly　　　エ. who-ev-er

3. ア. a-buse　　　　イ. o-ver　　　　　ウ. pho-to　　　　　エ. sun-shine

C Complete the following English sentences to match the Japanese.【表現と文法の知識】

(各3点)

1. 来る人はだれでも歓迎します。

   (　　　　　　　　) comes, we will welcome them.

2. 雄太は今年の文化祭で重要な役割を担っています。

   Yuta plays an important (　　　　　　　) in the cultural (　　　　　　) this year.

3. トムはとても難しい問題に挑戦しているので，後で話しかけるようにしてください。

   Tom is trying (　　　　　　　) a difficult question (　　　　　　　) I would like you to talk to him later.

D Arrange the words in the proper order to match the Japanese.【表現と文法の知識・技能】

(各3点)

1. ケイトは今日のイベントに責任があります。

   Kate (event / for / has / responsibility / today's).

   _____

2. 私は朝，深呼吸をしながら散歩するのが好きです。

   I (a deep breath / in / like / taking / the morning, / walking).

   _____

3. あなたのやったことが大変な問題につながりました。

   (did / led / terrible / to / trouble / what / you).

   _____

E Read the following passage and answer the questions below.

Wildlife tourism has caused some serious problems. Tourists and social media have responsibility for this. Whoever enjoys contact (1) animals on vacation just feels happy to be with them. Those people never think that their behaviors might hurt animals and the ecosystem. Moreover, (2)(on / seeing / social media, / the posted selfies / the site) visitors may hope to have the same experiences.

Recently, social media's role in the problem (3). A social media site started to show a pop-up warning when its users search, using hashtags like "#slothselfie" and "#koalaselfie."

Today, social media are such prevailing communication tools (4)(a great impact / can / have / that / they) anywhere. Even the single act of posting a photo can lead to animal abuse. Next time you take and post photos, think about how your photos might affect others.

1. 空所(1)に入る最も適当な語を選びなさい。【語彙と表現の知識】　　　　　　　　　（3点）

　　ア. for　　　　　　イ. of　　　　　　ウ. through　　　　エ. with

2. 下線部(2)の(　　)内の語句を適切に並べかえなさい。【表現と文法の知識】　　　　（3点）

_____

3. 空所(3)に入る最も適当な語句を選びなさい。【文法の知識】　　　　　　　　　　　（3点）

　　ア. has been recognized　　　　　イ. has been recognizing
　　ウ. has recognize　　　　　　　　エ. has recognized

4. 下線部(4)の(　　)内の語句を適切に並べかえなさい。【表現と文法の知識】　　　　（3点）

_____

5. 次の問いに英語で答えなさい。【内容についての思考力・判断力・表現力】　　　　　（各4点）

　(1) What has responsibility for the serious problems wildlife tourism has caused?

_____

　(2) What can lead to animal abuse?

_____

Information Please

 Part 1

/50

A Translate the English into Japanese and the Japanese into English. 【語彙の知識】（各 1 点）

1. wooden 形 A2　　[　　　　　]　2. fasten 動 B1　　[　　　　　]

3. hang 動 B1　　[　　　　　]　4. ＿＿＿＿＿＿ 副 B2　熱心に

5. device 名 B1　　[　　　　　]　6. ＿＿＿＿＿＿ 動 B2　…を提供する

B Choose the word whose underlined part is pronounced differently from the other three. 【発音の知識】　　　　　　　　　　　　　　（各 2 点）

1. ア. am<u>a</u>zing　　イ. ch<u>a</u>mber　　ウ. h<u>a</u>tred　　エ. m<u>a</u>gic

2. ア. imm<u>e</u>diately　イ. pr<u>e</u>cious　　ウ. pr<u>e</u>judice　　エ. tog<u>e</u>ther

3. ア. bom<u>b</u>　　イ. fas<u>t</u>en　　ウ. lau<u>gh</u>ter　　エ. mus<u>c</u>le

C Complete the following English sentences to match the Japanese. 【表現の知識】（各 3 点）

1. 父は私を肩車してくれました。

My father (　　　　　) me (　　　　　) on his shoulders.

2. 翌日，ティムは商用でパリに行きました。

The next day, Tim went to Paris (　　　　　) (　　　　　).

3. 私は両親にお金を出してと頼まなければなりませんでした。

I had to (　　　　　) my parents (　　　　　) money.

D Arrange the words in the proper order to match the Japanese. 【表現と文法の知識・技能】

（各 3 点）

1. 美術館から盗まれた絵はまだ発見されていない。

The paintings (been / found / from the museum / haven't / stolen) yet.

2. 郵便局のそばには，小さな灰色の教会が立っている。

(a little / beside / stands / the post office) gray church.

3. 彼は何でも知っていると思っている。

He thinks there is (does / he / know / not / nothing).

E Read the following passage and answer the questions below.

When Paul was quite young, his family had one of the first telephones in their neighborhood.

I remember well the wooden case (1)(fasten) to the wall on the stair landing. The receiver hung on the side of the box. I even remember the number —— 105. (2)(I / little / reach / the telephone / to / too / was), but used to listen eagerly when my mother talked to it. Once she lifted me up to speak to my father, who was away (3) business. Magic!

Then I discovered that somewhere inside that wonderful device lived an amazing person —— her name was "Information Please" and there was (4) she did not know.

My mother could ask her for anybody's number; when our clock ran down, Information Please immediately supplied the correct time.

1. 下線部(1)の語を適切な形に変えなさい。【文法の知識】　　　　　　　　　　（3点）

2. 下線部(2)の(　　)内の語句を適切に並べかえなさい。【表現と文法の知識】　　（3点）

3. 空所(3)，(4)に入る最も適当な語を選びなさい。【語彙と表現の知識】　　　（各3点）

   (3) ア. for　　　　イ. in　　　　　　ウ. on　　　　　エ. to
   (4) ア. anything　イ. none　　　　ウ. nothing　　エ. something

4. 次の問いに英語で答えなさい。【内容についての思考力・判断力・表現力】　　（各4点）
   (1) What was the telephone number of Paul's house?

   (2) What did Paul discover about the amazing person inside the wonderful device?

Information Please

Part 2

/50

A Translate the English into Japanese and the Japanese into English.【語彙の知識】(各1点)

1. amuse 動 B2　　　[　　　　　　]　2. suck 動 B2　　　[　　　　　　]

3. ＿＿＿＿ 名　足乗せ台　　　4. ＿＿＿＿ 名　送話口

5. bleed 動 B1　　　[　　　　　　]　6. warn 動 B1　　　[　　　　　　]

B Choose the word whose underlined part is pronounced differently from the other three.【発音の知識】(各2点)

1. ア. ab<u>o</u>ve　　　イ. cl<u>o</u>ck　　　ウ. disc<u>o</u>ver　　　エ. w<u>o</u>nderful

2. ア. cli<u>mb</u>　　　イ. de<u>v</u>ice　　　ウ. s<u>t</u>imulate　　　エ. <u>v</u>iolence

3. ア. gl<u>o</u>bally　　　イ. kn<u>ow</u>ledge　　　ウ. m<u>o</u>ment　　　エ. ph<u>o</u>ne

C Complete the following English sentences to match the Japanese.【表現の知識】(各3点)

1. その幼い女の子は何時間もおもちゃで遊んだ。

The little girl amused (　　　　　　) (　　　　　　) her toys for hours.

2. バスに間に合おうと走っただけで私は息が切れてしまいます。

Just (　　　　) (　　　　　　) the bus leaves me out of breath.

3. 子供たちを浜辺へ連れて行きましょう。

Let's (　　　　　) the kids (　　　　　) the beach.

D Arrange the words in the proper order to match the Japanese.【表現と文法の知識・技能】

(各3点)

1. ここには私の仕事はないようだ。

There (any work / be / doesn't / seem / to) for me here.

2. こぼれたミルクを嘆いてもむだだ(後悔先に立たず)。

There is (crying / no / over / spilled milk / use).

3. そのことを知らないのはあなただけのようだよ。

Everybody but (it / know / seems / to / you).

E Read the following passage and answer the questions below.

My first personal experience with this woman-in-the-receiver came one day while my mother was visiting a neighbor. (1)(a hammer / amusing / myself / with), I hit my finger. The pain was terrible, but there didn't seem to be much use (2)(cry) because there was no one home to hear me. I walked around the house sucking my finger, finally arriving at the landing. The telephone! Quickly I ran for the footstool and took it to the landing. Climbing up, I took the receiver and held it to my ear. "Information Please," I said into the mouthpiece just above my head.

A click or two, and a small, clear voice spoke into my ear. "Information."

"I hurt my fingerrrrr ——" I cried into the phone. The tears began running down, (3) I had an audience.

"Isn't your mother home?" (4)(come) the question.

"Nobody's home but me," I said.

"Are you bleeding?"

"No," I replied. "I hit it with the hammer and it hurts."

"Can you open your icebox?" she asked. I said I could.

"Then break off a little piece of ice and hold it on your finger. That will stop the hurt. Be careful when you use the ice pick," she warned. "And don't cry. You'll be all right."

1. 下線部(1)の(　　)内の語句を適切に並べかえなさい。【表現と文法の知識】　　　　　　　　　　　　(3 点)

2. 下線部(2), (4)の語を適切な形に変えなさい。【文法の知識】　　　　　　　　　　　(各 3 点)

　(2)

　(4)

3. 空所(3)に入る最も適当な語句を選びなさい。【表現の知識】　　　　　　　　　　(3 点)

　ア. by the time　　イ. every time　　ウ. in case　　エ. now that

4. 次の問いに英語で答えなさい。【内容についての思考力・判断力・表現力】　　　　　　(各 4 点)

　(1) When did Paul's first personal experience with the woman-in-the-receiver come?

　(2) What did she warn Paul when he asked for her help after hitting his finger with a hammer?

Information Please

Part 3

/50

A Translate the English into Japanese and the Japanese into English. 【語彙の知識】 (各1点)

1. _____ 名 B1　地理
2. explore 動 A2　[　　　　　]
3. _____ 名 B1　算数
4. grown-up 名 B2　[　　　　　]
5. soothe 動 B1　[　　　　　]
6. concern 名 A2　[　　　　　]

B Choose the word which has primary stress on a different syllable from the other three. 【アクセントの知識】 (各2点)

1. ア. con-cern　　　イ. cor-rect　　　ウ. ex-plore　　　エ. for-tune
2. ア. ca-nar-y　　　イ. per-son-al　　　ウ. rec-og-nize　　　エ. ter-ri-ble
3. ア. en-ter-tain-ment　イ. ge-og-ra-phy　ウ. in-flu-en-tial　エ. sit-u-a-tion

C Complete the following English sentences to match the Japanese. 【表現の知識】 (各3点)

1. この番号に電話して，サリーをお願いしますと言ってね。

   Phone this number and (　　　　　) (　　　　　) Sally.

2. 彼は東京で生まれたが，北海道で育った。

   He was born in Tokyo, but (　　　　　) (　　　　　) in Hokkaido.

3. それらのかばんを運ぶのを手伝いましょうか。

   Do you want me to (　　　　　) you (　　　　　) those bags?

D Arrange the words in the proper order to match the Japanese. 【文法の知識・技能】 (各3点)

1. 次の列車は何時か教えていただけませんか。

   Could you (is / me / tell / the next train / when)?

   _____

2. その当時，私は両親に言われたことをすべて信じていた。

   In those days I (believed / everything / me / my parents / told).

   _____

3. もし彼に遊び相手の子供がもう一人いれば，彼はもっと幸せなのに。

   If he (another child / had / play / to / with), he would be happier.

   _____

E Read the following passage and answer the questions below.

After that, I called Information Please for everything. (1)(asked / for / geography / help / I / my / with) and she told me (2) Philadelphia was, and the Orinoco —— the river I was going to explore when I grew up. She helped me with my arithmetic, and she told me that a pet chipmunk —— I had caught him in the park just the day before —— would eat fruit and nuts.

And there was the time (3)that our pet canary died. I called Information Please and told her the sad story. She listened, and then said the usual things grown-ups say to soothe a child. But I did not feel better: why should birds sing so beautifully and bring joy to whole families, only to end as a heap of feathers feet up, on the bottom of a cage?

She (4) have sensed my deep concern, for she said quietly, "Paul, always remember that there are other worlds to sing in."

Somehow I felt better.

1. 下線部(1)の(　　　)内の語を適切に並べかえなさい。【表現と文法の知識】　　　　　（3点）

....

2. 空所(2),（4)に入る最も適当な語を選びなさい。【語彙と表現の知識】　　　　　（各3点）

  (2) ア. what　　　　イ. whether　　　　ウ. where　　　　エ. why

  (4) ア. could　　　　イ. must　　　　ウ. should　　　　エ. would

3. 下線部(3)を別の語で言いかえなさい。【表現と文法の知識】　　　　　（3点）

  (　　　　　　　)

4. 次の問いに英語で答えなさい。【内容についての思考力・判断力・表現力】　　　　　（各4点）

  (1) What was the Orinoco?

....

  (2) What did Information Please tell Paul that a chipmunk would eat?

....

Information Please

Part 4

/50

A Translate the English into Japanese and the Japanese into English.【語彙の知識】（各 1 点）

1. fix 動 B1 [   ]   2. _____ 名 瞬間

3. scare 動 B1 [   ]   4. terrified 形 B1 [   ]

5. _____ 名 B2　オペレーター，電話交換手　6. repair 名 A2 [   ]

B Choose the word whose underlined part is pronounced differently from the other three.【発音の知識】（各 2 点）

1. ア. cancer　　　イ. chance　　　ウ. hammer　　　エ. later

2. ア. operator　　イ. problem　　　ウ. trouble　　　エ. volume

3. ア. quarter　　　イ. scare　　　ウ. score　　　エ. warn

C Complete the following English sentences to match the Japanese.【表現の知識】（各 3 点）

1. 彼ははしごから芝生の上へ落ちた。

He (   ) (   ) the ladder onto the grass.

2. 私たちはかつては仲のよい友達でしたが，もう友達ではありません。

We used to be good friends, but we are (   ) (   ) friends.

3. 私は政治にはまったく興味がありません。

I am not (   ) (   ) interested in politics.

D Arrange the words in the proper order to match the Japanese.【表現と文法の知識・技能】

（各 3 点）

1. 2 人の人が議論するとき，それぞれは相手が間違っていると確信している。

When two people argue, each (is / is / sure / that / the other person) wrong.

2. その火事を消すのに数時間かかった。

It took several hours (bring / control / the fire / to / under).

3. その子は犬の頭を軽くたたいた。

The child (a pat / gave / on / the head / the dog).

E Read the following passage and answer the questions below.

Another day I was at the telephone. "Information," said the now (1) voice.
"How do you spell fix?" I asked.

"Fix something? F-I-X."

At that instant my sister, trying to scare me, jumped off the stairs at me. I fell off the footstool, pulling the receiver out of the box. We were both terrified —— (2)(Information Please / longer / no / there / was), and I was not at all sure that I hadn't hurt her when I pulled the receiver out.

Minutes later there was a man at the door. "I'm a telephone repairman. I was working down the street and the operator said there might be some trouble at this number." He reached for the receiver in my hand. "What happened?"

I told him.

"Well, we can fix that in a minute or two." He opened the telephone box, did some repair work, and then spoke into the phone. "Hi, this is Pete. Everything's (3) control at 105. The kid's sister scared him and he pulled the cord out of the box."

He hung (4), smiled, gave me a pat on the head and walked out of the door.

1. 空所(1)に「聞き慣れた，よく知った」の意味の単語を答えなさい。【語彙と表現の知識】　（3点）

　　(　　　　　　)

2. 下線部(2)の(　　)内の語句を適切に並べかえなさい。【表現と文法の知識】　（3点）

3. 空所(3), (4)に入る最も適当な語を選びなさい。【表現の知識】　（各3点）

　(3) ア. before　　　イ. over　　　　ウ. under　　　　エ. without
　(4) ア. around　　　イ. down　　　　ウ. over　　　　エ. up

4. 次の問いに英語で答えなさい。【内容についての思考力・判断力・表現力】　（各4点）

　(1) Why was Paul terrified when he pulled the receiver out of the box?

　(2) Who was Pete?

Information Please

Part 5

/50

A Translate the English into Japanese and the Japanese into English.【語彙の知識】(各1点)

1. belong 動 A2 [　　　　　] 　 2. skinny 形 [　　　　　]

3. ＿＿＿＿＿ 名 B1 10代 　　　 4. childhood 名 A2 [　　　　　]

5. ＿＿＿＿＿ 形 B2 穏やかな 　 6. ＿＿＿＿＿ 動 A2 …をありがたく思う

B Choose the word which has primary stress on a different syllable from the other three.【アクセントの知識】(各2点)

1. ア. be-long 　　 イ. mo-ment 　　 ウ. re-spect 　　 エ. se-rene

2. ア. fi-nal-ly 　　 イ. mem-o-ry 　　 ウ. Pa-cif-ic 　　 エ. ter-ri-fy

3. ア. ap-pre-ci-ate 　 イ. cer-e-mo-ny 　 ウ. i-den-ti-ty 　 エ. se-cur-i-ty

B Complete the following English sentences to match the Japanese.【表現の知識】(各3点)

1. 私が最後にその村を訪れてから多くの変化が起こっている。

A lot of changes have (　　　　　) (　　　　　) since I last visited the village.

2. ジョージは転職しようかと考えている。

George is (　　　　　) (　　　　　) changing jobs.

3. 若い頃，彼はよくここらの林を散歩したものだ。

When he was young, he (　　　　　) (　　　　　) walk in these woods.

D Arrange the words in the proper order to match the Japanese.【表現と文法の知識・技能】

(各3点)

1. その皿の置き場所は，流しの上の戸棚です。

The plates (above / belong / in / the cupboard / the sink).

2. 離れて暮らすと，家族の大切さが改めて身にしみた。

Being away (appreciate / made / me / more / my family).

3. こんなことにこれ以上時間を無駄にするのはよしましょう。

Let's not (any / more / on / this / time / waste).

E Read the following passage and answer the questions below.

All this (1) in a small town in the Pacific Northwest. Then, when I was nine years old, we (2) the country to Boston —— and I missed Information Please very much. She (3) that old wooden box back home, and I somehow never thought of trying the tall, skinny new phone that sat on a small table in the hall.

Yet, as I (4) my teens, the memories of those childhood conversations never really left me; often in moments of doubt and worry I (5) recall the serene sense of security I had when I knew that I could call Information Please and get the right answer. I appreciated now (6)(and kind / how / patient, / she / understanding / was) to have wasted her time on a little boy.

1. 空所(1)〜(4)に入る適切な語句を下からそれぞれ選んで答えなさい。【表現と文法の知識】 （各2点）

    (1) ....

    (2) ....

    (3) ....

    (4) ....

    [belonged in, grew into, moved across, took place]

2. 空所(5)に入る最も適当な語を選びなさい。【表現と文法の知識】 （2点）

    ア. might イ. must ウ. should エ. would

3. 下線部(6)の(　　)内の語句を適切に並べかえなさい。【表現と文法の知識】 （2点）

    ....

4. 次の問いに英語で答えなさい。【内容についての思考力・判断力・表現力】 （各4点）

    (1) Where was the new telephone in Paul's new house in Boston?

    ....

    (2) When did Paul recall the childhood conversations with Information Please?

    ....

A Translate the English into Japanese and the Japanese into English.【語彙の知識】(各1点)

1. dial 動 B1 [   ] 2. miraculously 副 [   ]

3. _____ 動 A2 …を綴る 4. _____ 動 B1 返事をする

5. silly 形 A2 [   ] 6. _____ 名 A2 学期

B Choose the word whose underlined part is pronounced differently from the other three.【発音の知識】(各2点)

1. ア. br<u>ea</u>the   イ. f<u>ea</u>ther   ウ. inst<u>ea</u>d   エ. m<u>ea</u>nt

2. ア. f<u>o</u>llow   イ. h<u>o</u>nestly   ウ. pr<u>o</u>per   エ. w<u>o</u>nder

3. ア. d<u>ou</u>bt   イ. dr<u>ow</u>n   ウ. m<u>ou</u>se   エ. s<u>ou</u>l

C Complete the following English sentences to match the Japanese.【表現の知識】(各3点)

1. 子供たちは休暇を心待ちにしています。

The kids are (   ) (   ) to their vacation.

2. 私はシアトルの空港でたまたま旧友に出会った。

I (   ) (   ) an old friend at the airport in Seattle.

3. 近いうちに地震があるといううわさだ。

They say we'll have an earthquake one of (   ) (   ).

D Arrange the words in the proper order to match the Japanese.【表現と文法の知識】(各3点)

1. 彼女がだれにもさよならも言わずに帰って行ったのには驚いた。

I was surprised that she left (anyone / goodbye / saying / to / without).

_____

2. 隣の部屋から怒った声が聞こえてきた。

We (an angry voice / coming / from / heard / the next room).

_____

3. 親が子供を愛するのは当然のことである。

It is natural (for / love / parents / their children / to).

_____

E Read the following passage and answer the questions below.

A few years later, (1) my way west to college, my plane landed in Seattle. I had about half an hour before my plane left, and I spent (2)(minutes / on / or / so / the phone / 15) with my sister, who had a happy marriage there now. Then, really (3) thinking what I was doing, I dialed my hometown operator and said, "Information Please."

Miraculously, I heard again the small, clear voice I knew so well: "Information."

I hadn't planned this, but I heard myself saying, "Could you tell me, please, how to spell the word 'fix'?"

There was a long pause. Then came the softly (4)(speak) answer. "I guess," said Information Please, "that your finger must be all right by now."

I laughed. "So it's really still you. I wonder if you have any idea how much you meant to me during all that time ..."

"I wonder," she replied, "if you know how much you meant to me? I never had any children, and I (5)(forward / look / to / to / used / your calls). Silly, wasn't it?"

It didn't seem silly, but I didn't say so. Instead I told her how often I had thought of her over the years, and I asked if I could call her again when I came back to visit my sister after the first semester was over.

"Please do. Just ask for Sally."

"Goodbye, Sally." It sounded strange for Information Please to have a name. "If I run into any chipmunks, I'll tell them to eat fruit and nuts."

"Do that," she said. "And I expect one of these days you'll visit the Orinoco. Well, goodbye."

1. 空所(1), (3)に入る最も適当な語を選びなさい。【表現と文法の知識】　(各2点)

　(1) ア. for　　　イ. in　　　ウ. on　　　エ. to

　(3) ア. beside　　イ. over　　ウ. through　　エ. without

2. 下線部(2), (5)の(　　)内の語句を適切に並べかえなさい。【表現の知識】　(各3点)

　(2) _____

　(5) _____

3. 下線部(4)の語を適切な形に変えなさい。【文法の知識】　(2点)

_____

4. 次の問いに英語で答えなさい。【内容についての思考力・判断力・表現力】　(各4点)

　(1) Why was Paul in Seattle?

_____

　(2) What sounded strange to Paul when he was talking with Information Please?

_____

Information Please

/50

A Translate the English into Japanese and the Japanese into English.【語彙の知識】　（1点）

1. part-time 副 B1　　[　　　　　　　]　　2. ＿＿＿＿＿＿＿ 動 A2　死ぬ

3. minute 名 A1　　[　　　　　　　]　　4. ＿＿＿＿＿＿＿ 名 A1　伝言

5. almost 副 A1　　[　　　　　　　]　　6. ＿＿＿＿＿＿＿ 動 A1　…を意味する

B Choose the word which has primary stress on a different syllable from the other three.【アクセントの知識】　　（各2点）

1. ア. ef-fect　　　イ. mes-sage　　　ウ. pre-vent　　　エ. sup-port

2. ア. ad-vance　　イ. ef-fort　　　　ウ. in-sect　　　エ. mod-ern

3. ア. ca-nar-y　　イ. dif-fer-ent　　ウ. se-mes-ter　　エ. to-geth-er

C Complete the following English sentences to match the Japanese.【表現の知識】　（各3点）

1. 彼に伝言を残しますか。

Would you like to (　　　　　　　) a (　　　　　　　) for him?

2. ジョンの住所を書き留めましたか。

Did you (　　　　　　　) (　　　　　　　) John's address?

3. 旅行の計画はいつも前もって立てておくべきです。

You should always plan your trips (　　　　　　　) (　　　　　　　).

D Arrange the words in the proper order to match the Japanese.【表現と文法の知識・技能】

（各3点）

1. 残念ですが，あなたの申し込みはお断りさせていただきます。

I'm (sorry / tell / that / to / you) your application has been unsuccessful.

2. 私が何も言えないうちに，スティーヴは歩き去って行きました。

(anything / before / could / I / say), Steve walked away.

3. 私のおばあさんは，飲むのに自分専用のカップを持っていました。

My grandmother had (drink / her own cup / of / out / to).

E Read the following passage and answer the questions below.

Just three months later I was back again at the Seattle airport. A different voice answered, "Information," and I asked (1) Sally.

"Are you a friend?"

"Yes," I said. "An old friend."

"Then I'm sorry to have to tell you. Sally had only been working part-time in the last few years because she was ill. She died five weeks ago." But before I could hang up, she said, "Wait a minute. (2)(did / name / say / was / you / your) Willard?"

"Yes."

"Well, Sally left a message for you. She wrote it down."

"What was it?" I asked, almost knowing (3) advance what it would be.

"Here it is, I'll read it —— 'Tell him I still say there are other worlds to sing in. He'll know what I mean.' "

I thanked her and hung up. I (4)(do) know what Sally meant.

1. 空所(1), (3)に入る最も適当な語を選びなさい。【表現の知識】 (各3点)

   (1) ア. about   イ. for   ウ. to   エ. with

   (3) ア. for   イ. in   ウ. on   エ. under

2. 下線部(2)の(   )内の語を適切に並べかえなさい。【表現と文法の知識】 （3点）

3. 下線部(4)の語を適切な形に変えなさい。【文法の知識】 （3点）

4. 次の問いに英語で答えなさい。【内容についての思考力・判断力・表現力】 (各4点)

   (1) Why had Sally been working part-time in the last few years?

   (2) What was Sally's message for Paul?

Naomi Osaka's Interview after the 2018 U.S. Open

/50

A Translate the English into Japanese and the Japanese into English. 【語彙の知識】 (各1点)

1. _____ 形 B1　前の, 元の　　　2. interview 動 B1　[　　　　　　　]

3. cheer 動 A2　[　　　　　　]　　4. _____ 動 A2　終わる

5. _____ 名 A2　男性　　　　6. grateful 形 A2　[　　　　　　　]

B Choose the word whose underlined part is pronounced differently from the other three. 【発音の知識】　　　　　　　　　　　　　　　　　　(各2点)

1. ア. b<u>ea</u>t　　　イ. b<u>e</u>st　　　ウ. f<u>e</u>male　　　エ. S<u>e</u>rena

2. ア. gr<u>a</u>nd slam　イ. gr<u>a</u>teful　ウ. m<u>a</u>le　　　エ. pl<u>a</u>yer

3. ア. f<u>ir</u>st　　　イ. f<u>or</u>mer　　ウ. h<u>ur</u>t　　　エ. w<u>or</u>ld

C Complete the following English sentences to match the Japanese. 【表現と文法の知識】

(各3点)

1. チームメイトは大声を出して私を応援してくれた。

　　My teammates shouted and (　　　　　　) (　　　　　　) me.

2. 妻に出会えたことに感謝しています。

　　I (　　　　　) (　　　　　　) (　　　　　　) I could meet my wife.

3. 前の校長先生はとても厳しい人だった。

　　(　　　　　) (　　　　　　) principal was a very strict person.

D Arrange the words in the proper order to match the Japanese. 【表現と文法の知識・技能】

(各3点)

1. 今年祖父母に会うことができるのは嬉しい。

　　I am (glad / I / that / will) be able to see my grandparents this year.

　　_____

2. ここまでわざわざ会いに来てくれてありがとう。

　　(coming / for / thank / you) all the way here to see me.

　　_____

3. あなたのここでの仕事は中学生に数学を教えることです。

　　Your job here (is / math / teach / to) to junior high school students.

　　_____

E Read the following passage and answer the questions below.

In the U.S. Open finals, Naomi (1) Serena Williams, the former world number one player. She was interviewed after the match.

Naomi: I know that everyone was (2)(cheer) for Serena. I'm (3)(end / final match / had / our / sorry / to) like this. I just wanna say thank you for watching the match. Thank you.

Interviewer: The first Japanese player, male or female, from your country in history to win a Grand Slam final.

Naomi: (4)(dream / my / play / to / was / with) Serena in the U.S. Open finals. (5) I'm really glad that I was able to do that, and I'm really grateful I was able to play with her. Thank you!

1. 空所(1)に入る適当な語を選びなさい。【語彙と文法の知識】 （2点）

　　ア. beat　　　　　イ. beated　　　　ウ. beaten　　　　エ. beating

2. 下線部(2)の語を適切な形に変えなさい。【表現と文法の知識】 （2点）

　　　..

3. 下線部(3), (4)の(　　)内の語句を適切に並べかえなさい。【表現と文法の知識】 （各3点）

　　(3) ....

　　(4) ....

4. 空所(5)に入る最も適当な語を選びなさい。【語彙の知識】 （2点）

　　ア. Although　　　イ. Because　　　ウ. But　　　　エ. So

5. 次の問いに英語で答えなさい。【内容についての思考力・判断力・表現力】 （各4点）

　　(1) Who was interviewed after the match?

　　　..

　　(2) How did Naomi feel after she played with Serena Williams?

　　　..

Enjoy Making Delicious Banana Muffins

/50

A Translate the English into Japanese and the Japanese into English.【語彙の知識】(各1点)

1. _____ 名 B1　12個，1ダース　　2. _____ 名 A2　小麦粉

3. _____ 動　…を予熱する　　4. mixture 名 B2　[　　　　]

5. surface 名 B1　[　　　　]　　6. incredible 形 B1　[　　　　]

B Choose the word which has primary stress on a different syllable from the other three.【アクセントの知識】　　　　　　　　　　　　　　(各2点)

1. ア. but-ter　　イ. doz-en　　ウ. muf-fin　　エ. pre-heat

2. ア. fac-to-ry　　イ. fam-i-ly　　ウ. pri-va-cy　　エ. to-geth-er

3. ア. a-gain　　イ. mix-ture　　ウ. ov-en　　エ. sur-face

C Complete the following English sentences to match the Japanese.【表現の知識】(各3点)

1. 私たちは家に広い部屋を一つ加えた。

　We (　　　　　) a wide room (　　　　　) our house.

2. 彼女がなだめたので赤ん坊は泣きやんだ。

　She soothed the baby, and he (　　　　　) (　　　　　) .

3. 仕事の帰りに卵を一ダース買ってきてください。

　Please buy a (　　　　　) (　　　　　) eggs on your way home from work.

D Arrange the words in the proper order to match the Japanese.【表現と文法の知識・技能】

(各3点)

1. あなたの名前をリストに追加します。

　I will (add / name / the list / to / your).

　_____

2. トムが作ったスイーツは絶品でした。

　(cooked / incredible / some / sweets / Tom).

　_____

3. 私たちは，子供たちとこの料理を楽しく作りました。

　(enjoyed / making / my children / this food / we / with).

　_____

E Read the following passage and answer the questions below.

Easy Banana Muffin Recipe

Ingredients for a dozen muffins

Ⓓ×1/3 butter   Ⓓ×1/2 brown sugar   2 eggs

3 bananas   Ⓓ×1/4 milk   Ⓓ×2 flour

How to cook

1. Preheat the oven to 160℃.

2. (1) the butter and brown sugar in a bowl, and (2) them together.

3. (3) eggs, mashed bananas and milk.

4. Add the flour to the bowl, and mix all the ingredients.

5. Put the mixture in individual muffin cups.

6. (4) the muffins in the oven for 20-25 minutes. Stop (5)(bake) them when (6)their surfaces (t   ) light brown.

Comments

Vivian: Incredible. These muffins are (7)(   ) (   ).

Rachel: Easy to make! I made a dozen of them with my kids. They liked them so much!

1. 空所(1)〜(4)に入る最も適当な語をそれぞれ選びなさい。すべて小文字で示している。

【表現と文法の知識】(各1点)

ア. add   イ. bake   ウ. mix   エ. put

(1) (   )   (2) (   )   (3) (   )   (4) (   )

2. 下線部(5)の語を適切な形に変えなさい。【文法の知識】 (3点)

3. 下線部(6)が「表面がうす茶色になる」という意味になるように，空所に入る語を答えなさい。ただし，与えられた文字で始めること。【表現と文法の知識】 (2点)

(   )

4. 下線部(7)が，この料理が美味しいことを伝える文となるように，2語で補いなさい。

【内容についての思考力・判断力・表現力】(3点)

(   ) (   )

5. 次の問いに英語で答えなさい。【内容についての思考力・判断力・表現力】 (各4点)

(1) If we follow this recipe, what can we cook?

(2) How many muffins did Rachel make?

A New Map Symbol

/50

A Translate the English into Japanese and the Japanese into English.【語彙の知識】(各1点)

1. ＿＿＿＿＿＿＿＿ 名 B1　記念碑　　　2. torrential 形　　　[　　　　　　]

3. ＿＿＿＿＿＿＿＿ 名　　子孫　　　　4. erect 動　　　　[　　　　　　]

5. ＿＿＿＿＿＿＿＿ 名 A2　知恵　　　　6. warn 動 B1　　　[　　　　　　]

B Choose the word which has primary stress on a different syllable from the other three.【アクセントの知識】(各2点)

1. ア. dam-age 　　　イ. e-rect 　　　　ウ. sym-bol 　　　エ. wis-dom

2. ア. dis-as-ter 　　イ. gov-ern-ment 　ウ. mon-u-ment 　エ. res-i-dent

3. ア. de-scend-ant 　イ. neigh-bor-hood 　ウ. re-mem-ber 　エ. tor-ren-tial

C Complete the following English sentences to match the Japanese.【表現と文法の知識】

(各3点)

1. AI は「人工知能」を表す。

　AI (　　　　　　　) (　　　　　　　　　) "Artificial Intelligence."

2. 彼女はその病気から来る激しい痛みに苦しんだ。

　She (　　　　　　　) terrible pain from the disease.

3. 犬は好きではなかったですよね。

　You don't like dogs, (　　　　　　) (　　　　　　)?

D Arrange the words in the proper order to match the Japanese.【表現と文法の知識・技能】

(各3点)

1. 私は放課後，父に車で迎えに来てほしかった。

　I (my father / pick / to / wanted) me up after school.

2. 私は彼女が1日に飲むコーヒーの量に驚いている。

　I am surprised (coffee / how / much / she) drinks in a day.

3. 兄はある女の子とデートをしたと言った。

　My brother (had / he / said / that) had a date with a girl.

E Read the following passage and answer the questions below.

Manabu: This is a new map symbol. It stands for a natural disaster monument.

Vivian: Um, (1) do we need a new symbol now?

Manabu: In recent years, torrential rains have caused floods. Some areas have suffered serious damage, and people have (2)(lose) their homes and families.

Vivian: Ah! It sounds terrible.

Manabu: I think so, too. Anyway, people in the past wanted their descendants to remember their sad experiences. They erected monuments which told where past disasters had happened and how (3)(caused / damage / had / much / they).

Vivian: The Japanese government has used the wisdom of people in the past to create a new map symbol, (4)?

Manabu: That's right. (5)(did / that / the government / to / warn) residents about the risks of disasters in their neighborhoods.

Vivian: That sounds like a great idea!

1. 空所(1)に入る最も適当な語を選びなさい。【表現の知識】　　　　　　　　　　　　　（2点）

　　　ア. what　　　　　　イ. when　　　　　　ウ. where　　　　　エ. why

2. 下線部(2)の語を適切な形に変えなさい。【文法の知識】　　　　　　　　　　　　　　（2点）

　　　　..

3. 下線部(3), (5)の(　　)内の語句を適切に並べかえなさい。【表現と文法の知識】　　（各3点）

　　(3) ....

　　(5) ....

4. 空所(4)に入る最も適当な語句を選びなさい。【語彙と表現の知識】　　　　　　　　　（2点）

　　　ア. does it　　　　　イ. doesn't it　　　　ウ. has it　　　　　エ. hasn't it

5. 次の問いに英語で答えなさい。【内容についての思考力・判断力・表現力】　　　　（各4点）

　　(1) Manabu shows Vivian a new map symbol. What does it stand for?

　　　..

　　(2) Why did people in the past erect monuments?

　　　..

Breaking Bread Together; Sharing Different Cultures

/50

A Translate the English into Japanese and the Japanese into English.【語彙の知識】(各1点)

1. _____ 名 A2 記念日，…周年

2. immigrant 名 B2 [　　　　　]

3. _____ 名 B1 やる気，熱意

4. recipe 名 B2 [　　　　　]

5. _____ 名 　ベーグル

6. background 名 A2 [　　　　　]

B Choose the word which has primary stress on a different syllable from the other three.【アクセントの知識】(各2点)

1. ア. com-mu-ni-ty 　イ. ex-pe-ri-ence 　ウ. in-cred-i-ble 　エ. pop-u-la-tion

2. ア. ag-ri-cul-ture 　イ. ed-u-ca-tion 　ウ. grad-u-a-tion 　エ. mo-ti-va-tion

3. ア. back-ground 　イ. ba-gel 　ウ. re-port 　エ. sun-shine

C Complete the following English sentences to match the Japanese.【表現と文法の知識】

(各3点)

1. 希美は1992年にニューヨークに着きました。

Nozomi (　　　　　) (　　　　　　　) New York in 1992.

2. この公園は自然であふれています。

This park is (　　　　　) (　　　　　　　) nature.

3. 謙二は，自分のお店がみんなから愛されることを望んでいます。

Kenji (　　　　　) (　　　　　　　) his store is loved by everyone.

D Arrange the words in the proper order to match the Japanese.【表現と文法の知識・技能】

(各3点)

1. このトラはこの公園で最も有名な動物の一つです。

This tiger (animals / in / is / most famous / of the / one / this park).

2. 菜緒はイベントを催すことを計画しています。

Nao (an event / hold / is / planning / to).

3. 優佳は彼をショーに誘った。

Yuka (go / him / invited / the show / to / to).

E Read the following passage and answer the questions below.

Good evening. This is our top story tonight.

Today, in Montreal, one of the city's favorite stores celebrated its 60th anniversary. The store (1)(open) by a young immigrant from Poland, who arrived in Canada in 1952. This Pole was full of motivation, and he wanted to bring his love for bread to (2)his new home. The local community (3) him and his recipes. His bagels have become very popular in the city.

To show its gratitude, the store held a special event for the local community. The family-run business invited people to come and learn (4) to make its delicious bagels. The event brought people of different cultures and backgrounds together. The owner hopes that people from a lot of different backgrounds share their love for bagels.

1. 下線部(1)の語を適切な形に変えなさい。2語以上になることもあります。【文法の知識】 （3点）

　　　..

2. 下線部(2)のある国はどこか。英語で答えなさい。【内容についての思考力・判断力・表現力】 （3点）

　　　..

3. 空所(3), (4)に入る最も適当な語を選びなさい。【表現と文法の知識】 （各3点）

　　(3) ア. imported　　　イ. invited　　　ウ. used　　　エ. welcomed
　　(4) ア. how　　　イ. what　　　ウ. when　　　エ. why

4. 次の問いに英語で答えなさい。【内容についての思考力・判断力・表現力】 （各4点）

　　(1) What did one of the city's favorite stores celebrate?

　　..

　　(2) What does the owner hope?

　　..

Cats or Dogs?

/50

A Translate the English into Japanese and the Japanese into English.【語彙の知識】(各1点)

1. prefer 動 A2　　　　[　　　　　　] 2. ＿＿＿＿＿ 名 A1 隣人，近所の人

3. ＿＿＿＿＿ 名 B2 治療，療法 4. rescue 名 B1　　[　　　　　　]

5. sociable 形 B2　　[　　　　　　] 6. ＿＿＿＿＿ 形 B2 愛情深い，優しい

B Choose the word whose underlined part is pronounced differently from the other three.【発音の知識】

(各2点)

1. ア. <u>a</u>ffectionate　　イ. <u>e</u>ven　　ウ. h<u>ea</u>lthy　　エ. th<u>e</u>rapy

2. ア. c<u>are</u>　　イ. pref<u>er</u>　　ウ. sh<u>are</u>　　エ. wh<u>ere</u>

3. ア. ab<u>o</u>ve　　イ. c<u>o</u>ver　　ウ. s<u>o</u>ciable　　エ. tr<u>ou</u>ble

C Complete the following English sentences to match the Japanese.【表現と文法の知識】

(各3点)

1. 私は，言われたようにそのボタンを押しただけです。

I just pushed the button (　　　　　) (　　　　　) (　　　　　) told to.

2. 母は人の面倒を見るのが好きなんです。

My mother likes (　　　　　) (　　　　　) (　　　　　) other people.

3. スマートフォンがあれば，海外旅行をするのがずっと楽ですよ。

If you have a smartphone, it is (　　　　　) (　　　　　) to travel abroad.

D Arrange the words in the proper order to match the Japanese.【表現と文法の知識・技能】

(各3点)

1. ロッカーを掃除するのを手伝ってあげるよ。

I will (clean / help / locker / you / your).

＿＿＿＿＿＿＿＿＿＿＿＿＿＿＿＿＿＿＿＿＿＿＿＿＿＿＿＿＿＿＿＿

2. たくさん面倒をかけてしまいすみません。

I'm sorry I (caused / have / much / trouble / you).

＿＿＿＿＿＿＿＿＿＿＿＿＿＿＿＿＿＿＿＿＿＿＿＿＿＿＿＿＿＿＿＿

3. いくらか運動をすれば，気分がよくなるよ。

(make / some exercise / will / you) feel better.

＿＿＿＿＿＿＿＿＿＿＿＿＿＿＿＿＿＿＿＿＿＿＿＿＿＿＿＿＿＿＿＿

E Read the following passage and answer the questions below.

Which opinion do you agree with? Why?

(1)(as / cats / having / pets / will) cause you less trouble. You don't have to take your cat for a walk. When cats go to the bathroom, they just take care of themselves by covering their poo up. Also, having a cat won't put you in any trouble with your neighbors because cats won't bark at or jump on other people as dogs sometimes (2)do.

First of all, dogs can be trained to help human beings in many ways. We have therapy dogs, guide dogs, and even rescue dogs. Moreover, walking your dog every day (3)(healthy / help / stay / will surely / you). (4), dogs are much more sociable and affectionate toward us than cats. You know, dogs have long been called "man's best friend."

1. 下線部(1), (3)の(　　)内の語句を適切に並べかえなさい。【表現と文法の知識】　　　　(各3点)

(1) ....

(3) ....

2. 下線部(2)は何を指していますか。英語で答えなさい。【内容についての思考力・判断力・表現力】（3点）

....

3. 空所(4)に入る最も適当な語(句)を選びなさい。【語彙と文法の知識】　　　　　　　（3点）

ア. Above all　　　イ. However　　　ウ. Instead　　　エ. Still

4. 次の問いに英語で答えなさい。【内容についての思考力・判断力・表現力】　　　　(各4点)

(1) When cats go to the bathroom, how do they take care of themselves?

....

(2) What have dogs been called?

....

A Drone Changed My Life

/50

A Translate the English into Japanese and the Japanese into English. 【語彙の知識】(各1点)

1. ＿＿＿＿＿ 名 B1 ビデオクリップ
2. ＿＿＿＿＿ 副 B1 ついに, 結局は
3. ＿＿＿＿＿ 動 B2 …を輸入する
4. component 名 B2 [   ]
5. competition 名 A2 [   ]
6. confidence 名 B1 [   ]

B Choose the word which has primary stress on a different syllable from the other three. 【アクセントの知識】(各2点)

1. ア. ar-ti-cle　　イ. com-po-nent　　ウ. dis-as-ter　　エ. pi-an-o
2. ア. com-pe-ti-tion　イ. il-lus-tra-tion　ウ. sit-u-a-tion　エ. tech-nol-o-gy
3. ア. cam-er-a　　イ. com-pa-ny　　ウ. com-po-nent　　エ. con-fi-dence

C Complete the following English sentences to match the Japanese. 【表現と文法の知識】(各3点)

1. この機械で何を作ったの？
   What did you (   ) (   ) this machine?
2. ピーターはそのアイドルに恋をした。
   Peter (   ) in love (   ) the idol.
3. 淳はペンギンについて勉強を始めた。
   Jun (   ) (   ) about penguins.

D Arrange the words in the proper order to match the Japanese. 【表現と文法の知識・技能】(各3点)

1. あなたがサッカーにはまるきっかけは何でしたか。
   (did / get / how / into / soccer / you)?

   ＿＿＿＿＿＿＿＿＿＿

2. あなたが間違っていると思う人はほとんどいません。
   (are / few / people / think / wrong / you).

   ＿＿＿＿＿＿＿＿＿＿

3. 私はバスケットボールから多くのことを学びました。
   I (a lot / basketball / from / learned).

   ＿＿＿＿＿＿＿＿＿＿

E Read the following passage and answer the questions below.

> *Interviewer:* Please (1)(about / flying drones / got / how / into / me / tell / you).
>
> *Tomoki:* When I was in junior high school, I saw an exciting video clip made with drones (2) the Internet. After that, I started learning about drones. Eventually, I imported the components for a drone myself.
>
> *Interviewer:* Wow. Why did you fall in love with drones?
>
> *Tomoki:* At school, I was shy and had few friends. Flying drones by myself was a lot of fun. I started going out to fly drones (3) keeping myself at home. Drones changed my life!
>
> *Interviewer:* (4)
>
> *Tomoki:* I took part in international competitions and performed well. That gave me confidence. I started a drone company with my father and I stopped staying at home.
>
> *Interviewer:* What did you learn from drones?
>
> *Tomoki:* Everybody has a chance to meet something that can change their life.
>
> *Interviewer:* Well, thank you very much.

1. 下線部(1)の(　　)内の語句を適切に並べかえなさい。【表現と文法の知識】　　　　　　　　（3点）

　　　..

2. 空所(2)に入る最も適当な語を選びなさい。【語彙の知識】　　　　　　　　　　　　　　　　（3点）

　　　ア. at　　　　　　　イ. in　　　　　　　ウ. on　　　　　　　エ. with

3. 空所(3)に入る最も適当な語句を選びなさい。【表現の知識】　　　　　　　　　　　　　　　（3点）

　　　ア. in spite of　　　イ. instead of　　　ウ. owing to　　　エ. regarding to

4. 空所(4)に入る最も適当な表現を選びなさい。【内容についての思考力・判断力・表現力】　　　（3点）

　　　ア. I know.　　　　イ. Tell me more.　　ウ. What do you join?

5. 次の問いに英語で答えなさい。【内容についての思考力・判断力・表現力】　　　　　　　　（各4点）

　　　(1) What did Tomoki see when he was in junior high school?

　　　..

　　　(2) What did Tomoki start with his father?

　　　..

Art Doctors

A Translate the English into Japanese and the Japanese into English. 【語彙の知識】(各1点)

1. studio 名 B1　　　[　　　　　　] 2. _____ 形　　壊れやすい, もろい

3. _____ 動 B2　　…を扱う　 4. conserve 動　　[　　　　　　　]

5. _____ 名 B1　　部門, 部署　 6. conservation 名 B1　　[　　　　　　　]

B Choose the word which has primary stress on a different syllable from the other three. 【アクセントの知識】　　　　　　　　　　　　　　　　　　　　(各2点)

1. ア. art-ist　　　イ. con-serve　　　ウ. doc-tor　　　エ. frag-ile

2. ア. de-part-ment　イ. es-sen-tial　　ウ. mu-se-um　　エ. stu-di-o

3. ア. ad-di-tion-al　イ. con-ser-va-tion　ウ. con-ser-va-tor　エ. o-rig-i-nal

C Complete the following English sentences to match the Japanese. 【語彙と表現の知識】

(各3点)

1. ガラスは割れやすいから落とさないように気をつけて。

　 Glass is (　　　　　　) so be careful not to drop it.

2. 彼は年をとるにつれて, 頑固になった。

　 (　　　　　　) he grew older, he became more stubborn.

3. 生徒たちは英語のスキルを伸ばそうとしています。

　 The students are (　　　　　　) (　　　　　　) improve their English skills.

D Arrange the words in the proper order to match the Japanese. 【表現と文法の知識・技能】

(各3点)

1. 何よりもまず, 現実的な目標を設定することが不可欠だ。

　 First of all, (essential / is / it / to) set a realistic goal.

2. なぜ彼はそのような扱いをされなければならなかったのでしょうか。

　 Why did he (be / have / treated / to) that way?

3. 風邪を治すのに最もよい方法は, よく眠ることだよ。

　 (best / get / the / to / way) over your cold is to sleep well.

E Read the following passage and answer the questions below.

Have you ever (1)(hear) that there are doctors in the art world? Kikuko Iwai, an art conservator, has restored valuable paintings, such as Claude Monet's *Water Lilies* and Vincent van Gogh's *Sunflowers*. She has also restored some *chigiri-e* paintings.

Iwai says, "Artworks are alive, so they (2)(aging / are / as / passes / time). (3)They are extremely fragile and need to be treated carefully. It is essential to keep their original quality. I have to choose the best way to conserve the painting (4)(changing / that / the artist / the original message / without) wanted to deliver."

Iwai worries that very (5) Japanese museums have a special department for art conservation. Kie, her daughter, has decided to become an art conservator, too. Kie aims to follow her mother's path as an "art doctor."

1. 下線部(1)の語を適切な形に変えなさい。【文法の知識】 （2点）

_____

2. 下線部(2), (4)の(   )内の語句を適切に並べかえなさい。【表現と文法の知識】 （各3点）

  (2) _____

  (4) _____

3. 下線部(3)は何を指していますか。英語で答えなさい。【内容についての思考力・判断力・表現力】 （2点）

_____

4. 空所(5)に入る最も適当な語(句)を選びなさい。【語彙と文法の知識】 （2点）

  ア. a few   イ. a little   ウ. few   エ. little

5. 次の問いに英語で答えなさい。【内容についての思考力・判断力・表現力】 （各4点）

  (1) Why do we need to treat artworks carefully?

_____

  (2) What has Kie decided to become in the future?

_____

A Monument Calling for Peace

/50

A Translate the English into Japanese and the Japanese into English.【語彙の知識】(各1点)

1. _____ 名 B1 彫刻　　　2. _____ 動 A2 重さが…ある

3. stability 名 B2　[　　　　　]　4. coexistence 名　[　　　　　]

5. inscribe 動 B1　[　　　　　]　6. _____ 名 B1 破壊, 破滅

B Choose the word which has primary stress on a different syllable from the other three.【アクセントの知識】　(各2点)

1. ア. ben-e-fit　　イ. im-pres-sion　　ウ. mon-u-ment　　エ. sym-bol-ize

2. ア. ed-u-ca-tion　イ. pop-u-la-tion　ウ. sit-u-a-tion　エ. sta-bil-i-ty

3. ア. in-scribe　　イ. lo-cate　　ウ. sculp-ture　　エ. weap-on

C Complete the following English sentences to match the Japanese.【表現・文法の知識】

(各3点)

1. このタワーは田園地帯にある。

This tower is (　　　　　　) in a rural (　　　　　　).

2. このモニュメントは高さ2メートルある。

This monument is two (　　　　　　) (　　　　　　).

3. このワインは日本の有名な俳優が作りました。

This wine was made (　　　　　　) a famous Japanese (　　　　　　).

D Arrange the words in the proper order to match the Japanese.【表現と文法の知識・技能】

(各3点)

1. 瑞希は授業中にメモを取りました。

(during / Mizuki / notes / the class / took).

_____

2. 先生は私の机の前に立った。

(front / in / my desk / of / stood / the teacher).

_____

3. そのルールはみんなが時代遅れだと思ったので廃止されました。

(abolished / because / everyone / it / the rule / thought / was / was) out of date.

_____

E Read the following passage and answer the questions below.

(1)On the two anniversary of Pope John Paul II's visit to Hiroshima in 1981, the Monument for Peace was unveiled. The monument is located in the lobby of the Hiroshima Peace Memorial Museum. The sculpture was made by (2)(an / artist / born in / Hiroshima / Italy-based). It is 3 meters high, 1.8 meters wide, and 0.9 meters long. And it weighs 6 tons. It symbolizes the world's stability, harmony and coexistence.

John Paul II left a powerful impression (3) Japanese citizens during his visit. The Pope (4) a speech in front of the Cenotaph for the A-bomb Victims on February 25, 1981. He read his appeal aloud in nine languages, including Japanese. His words called on the world to abolish nuclear weapons. A passage from his appeal is inscribed on the monument, both in Japanese and in English.

1. 下線部(1)には文法・語法的に間違いのある個所が1つあります。指摘して正しなさい。

【表現と文法の知識】（3点）

　　誤) _____ →正) _____

2. 下線部(2)の(　　)内の語句を適切に並べかえなさい。【表現の知識】　　　　　　（3点）

　　_____

3. 空所(3), (4)に入る最も適当な語を選びなさい。【表現と文法の知識】　　　　（各3点）

　　(3) ア. at　　　　イ. in　　　　ウ. on　　　　エ. to
　　(4) ア. left　　　イ. made　　　ウ. spoke　　　エ. talked

4. 次の問いに英語で答えなさい。【内容についての思考力・判断力・表現力】　　　（各4点）

　　(1) What does the sculpture symbolize?

　　(2) How many languages were used to inscribe a passage from John Paul II's appeal?

　　_____

Your Ideas May Change Society

/50

A Translate the English into Japanese and the Japanese into English.【語彙の知識】(各1点)

1. ＿＿＿＿＿ 名　活性化　　　　　2. ＿＿＿＿＿ 名 B1　参加者

3. application 名 B1　[　　　　　]　4. propose 動 B1　[　　　　　]

5. promotion 名 B1　[　　　　　]　6. ＿＿＿＿＿ 名　育児, 保育

B Choose the word which has primary stress on a different syllable from the other three.【アクセントの知識】(各2点)

1. ア. child-care　　イ. cur-rent　　ウ. pam-phlet　　エ. pro-pose

2. ア. con-tin-ue　　イ. de-vel-op　　ウ. pro-mo-tion　　エ. re-gion-al

3. ア. ap-pli-ca-tion　イ. ed-u-ca-tion　ウ. par-tic-i-pant　エ. pop-u-la-tion

C Complete the following English sentences to match the Japanese.【表現の知識】(各3点)

1. 高校を卒業したら, 何をしたいですか。

What do you want to do after you (　　　　　) (　　　　　) high school?

2. このアンケートに記入していただきたい。

We would like you to (　　　　　) (　　　　　) this questionnaire.

3. 英語の申込書をもらえますか。

May I have an (　　　　　) (　　　　　) in English?

D Arrange the words in the proper order to match the Japanese.【表現と文法の知識・技能】

(各3点)

1. 駅に近いこともあって, そのアパートは人気があります。

The apartment is popular (because / is / it / partly) located near the station.

_____

2. 長い間勉強させられ続けてきたから, 勉強するのは嫌いなんです。

I don't like studying because I (be / continued / have / to) forced to study for a long time.

_____

3. 彼女にもう一度チャンスを与えるべきだ。

One more chance (be / given / should / to) her.

_____

E Read the following passage and answer the questions below.

High School Student Regional Town Vitalization Idea Contest

Our town has several challenges (1) the moment. (2), the population here has continued to decrease, partly because a lot of younger people leave here for jobs or higher education when they graduate from school.

Your ideas can change this situation (3)(achieve / and / help / to) future development of our town.

Participants will give a presentation at the town cultural center on February 15. Special prizes (4)(awarded / be / the winners / to / will)!

Application method: Choose one of the issues below and propose your ideas. Fill out the (5)(require) online form by January 31.

The current challenges of our town:

1. Health and welfare　　　　2. Cultural promotion
3. Childcare support　　　　4. Education
5. Environmental measures　　6. Other

1. 空所(1), (2)に入る最も適当な語(句)を選びなさい。【語彙と表現の知識】　　　(各2点)

　(1) ア. at　　　　　イ. in　　　　　ウ. on　　　　　エ. to
　(2) ア. For example　イ. Fortunately　ウ. However　エ. Nevertheless

2. 下線部(3), (4)の(　　)内の語句を適切に並べかえなさい。【表現の知識】　　　(各3点)

　(3) _____
　(4) _____

3. 下線部(5)の語を適切な形に変えなさい。【語彙と文法の知識】　　　(2点)

　_____

4. 次の問いに英語で答えなさい。【内容についての思考力・判断力・表現力】　　　(各4点)

　(1) Why do many young people leave the town?

　_____

　(2) What will the participants in the contest do at the town cultural center?

　_____

Maria Island Pledge

/50

A Translate the English into Japanese and the Japanese into English. 【語彙の知識】 (各1点)

1. _____ 名 誓約　　　　2. _____ 名 B1 生息地

3. adorable 形 B1　　[　　　　　　]　　4. _____ 名 A2 行動

5. influence 名 A2　　[　　　　　　]　　6. protect 動 B1　　[　　　　　　]

B Choose the word which has primary stress on a different syllable from the other three. 【アクセントの知識】 (各2点)

1. ア. con-ser-va-tion　イ. en-vi-ron-ment　ウ. ex-pe-ri-ence　エ. par-tic-i-pate

2. ア. how-ev-er　　　イ. o-pin-ion　　　ウ. pop-u-lar　　　エ. re-mem-ber

3. ア. con-fuse　　　イ. pro-tect　　　ウ. re-spect　　　エ. wild-life

C Complete the following English sentences to match the Japanese. 【表現の知識】 (各3点)

1. 私はこの経験を決して忘れません。

I will never (　　　　　　　　) this (　　　　　　　　).

2. この街に住む人の数が増えています。

The (　　　　　　　　) of people living in this city is (　　　　　　　　).

3. インターネットは子供に悪い影響を与えると考える人がいます。

Some people think the Internet (　　　　　　　　) a bad (　　　　　　　　) on children.

D Arrange the words in the proper order to match the Japanese. 【表現と文法の知識・技能】

(各3点)

1. 昨日トムと話をしたのは楽しかったです。

I (enjoyed / talking / Tom / with / yesterday).

_____

2. 私たちの英語の先生は私たちに留学することを勧めた。

(abroad / encouraged / English teacher / our / study / to / us).

_____

3. 毎日運動をすることを誓います。

I (do / every day / exercise / pledge / some / to).

_____

E Read the following passage and answer the questions below.

Maria Island —— That Is Their Home

Maria Island sits (1) the East Coast of Tasmania, Australia. It has a rich natural environment. Visitors enjoy seeing wildlife in its natural habitat. It is a special experience for everyone who visits. Recently, (2)some photos visitors have posted on social media have made the island known to many other people. The number of tourists has increased greatly.

One of the most popular animals among the tourists visiting the island (3) the wombat, an adorable and friendly animal. Sadly, however, some people don't recognize that they are visiting the animals' home. (4)They often get too close to the wombats. The human behavior has a bad influence on the animals' health.

Nowadays, visitors to the island are encouraged to sign the Maria Island Pledge. The pledge begins as follows: "I take this pledge to respect and protect the furred and feathered residents of Maria. I will remember you are wild and pledge to keep you this way."

1. 空所(1)に入る最も適当な語を選びなさい。【語彙の知識】　　　　　　（3点）

　　ア. of　　　　　　　イ. off　　　　　　　ウ. on　　　　　　　エ. out

2. 下線部(2)の主語と述語動詞を指定された語数で抜き出しなさい。【文法の知識】　（完答3点）

　　主語（1語）: _____　　述語動詞（2語）: _____

3. 空所(3)に入る最も適当な be-動詞を答えなさい。【表現と文法の知識】　　（3点）

　　（　　　　）

4. 下線部(4)を日本語に訳しなさい。【内容についての思考力・判断力・表現力】　（3点）

　　_____

5. 次の問いに英語で答えなさい。【内容についての思考力・判断力・表現力】　（各4点）

　　(1) What has a rich natural environment?

　　_____

　　(2) What are visitors to Maria Island encouraged to do?

　　_____